Transference and Countertransference

Transference and Countertransference

A Therapeutic Method for Application in Everyday Psychosocial Counselling

Fee van Delft

international publishing

Published, sold and distributed by Eleven International Publishing
P.O. Box 85576
2508 CG The Hague
The Netherlands
Tel.: +31 70 33 070 33
Fax: +31 70 33 070 30
e-mail: sales@budh.nl
www.elevenpub.com

Sold and distributed in USA and Canada
International Specialized Book Services
920 NE 58th Avenue, Suite 300
Portland, OR 97213-3786, USA
Tel: 1-800-944-6190 (toll-free)
Fax: +1 503 280-8832
orders@isbs.com
www.isbs.com

Eleven International Publishing is an imprint of Boom uitgevers Den Haag.

ISBN 978-94-90947-50-7

Translated by Bridget Ashburn.

© 2012 F. van Delft | Eleven International Publishing, The Hague

This publication is protected by international copyright law.
All rights reserved. No part of this publication may be reproduced, stored in a retrieval system, or transmitted in any form or by any means, electronic, mechanical, photocopying, recording or otherwise, without the prior permission of the publisher.

Printed in the Netherlands.

Preface

Many years ago, whilst a colleague and I were working on our first educational textbook, I was fortunate enough to receive the guidance of an experienced senior editor, Jan van Haaren. Throughout this process – neither my colleague nor I had ever written a book before – Jan offered us constructive criticism in a way which encouraged us and made us think. He never gave us the feeling that we were on the wrong track or that we were putting incomprehensible sentences together, although this was quite often the case; what he did was to make the kind of comments and ask the sort of questions which enabled us to make the discovery for ourselves. He was always enthusiastic and inspiring. On more than one occasion, whilst waiting at the station together for the trains which would take us to our different corners of the globe, my editor and I would voluntarily let a train go by so that we could finish one of our animated discussions: a fairly huge risk, considering the reliability of the rail network! I had a secret urge to introduce him to my mother: my father had died a few years earlier. I thought they would make such a nice couple!
After this first book had gone to press, Jan suggested that I might think about writing a book on the theme of *transference* and *countertransference*. Not long after this Jan van Haaren died, unexpectedly and prematurely. The idea of writing a book about transference was put to one side and it was some time later that I was asked for a second time, and now by Jan's successor, what I thought about writing a book about transference. Whilst I was sitting musing to myself over this theme one day, the process of writing my very first book came into my mind and I started to think about Jan van Haaren. Suddenly I realized it: I had been in a transference situation with my inspiring senior editor! It wasn't that I had seen him as a prospective partner for my mother: I had wanted him as a 'father'. He had met in me perfectly the child's need: 'to be understood and encouraged'. He had fulfilled a longing which I had projected onto him and this is what we call transference.

I would like to thank Jan for his trust and his inspiration. I thank Yvonne Rol for going through this book with me and for her fruitful suggestions. My thanks to Joke, Ron, Bianca, Rose, Sandra, Cleotha, Joan, Rinalda, Jo-Anne, Renee, Kathy, Esther, Berbe, Marijke, Dineke, Mirjam, Alexandra, Louis, Hans, Elze, Deborah, Machteld, Silvia, Ria, Avis, my friends and (former) students, for their valuable contribution. Their honest, open and often astonishing stories bring vividness and clarity to what otherwise would just be dry theory.

Contents

Introduction 9

1   An initial exploration of the terms transference and countertransference 13
1.1   Projection and transference 14
1.2   Transference and countertransference 15
        1.2.1   Recognizing similarities in a situation or a person 17
1.3   Professional guidance 19

2   **Transference and countertransference** 23
2.1   The psychoanalytical approach 23
2.2   Transference 28
2.3   Resistance 30
2.4   Countertransference 34
2.5   Some general comments about transference and countertransference 37
2.6   Transformation processes and transference 40

3   **Transference and countertransference seen from the child-position** 45
3.1   'To be or not to be' 45
        3.1.1   Self-awareness 47
        3.2.1   Self-image mirrored 49
3.2   The child position within Transactional Analysis 50
        3.2.1   The TA perspective on transference 57
        3.2.2   The TA perspective on countertransference 60
        3.2.3   The little professor 62
3.3   Conscious and unconscious projection 68
3.4   Transference and family role 70
3.5   Positive and negative transference 73

4	Defining features in daily practice	75
4.1	Working with objectives	76
4.2	Continuous interaction	77
4.3	Punctuation	81
4.4	Content and context	83
4.5	Closeness and distance	86
4.6	Dependency	89

5	The professional conduct and skills of the practitioner	95
5.1	Transference? Countertransference?	96
	5.1.1 An attempt at clarification	97
5.2	(Self)knowledge, (self)consciousness and (self)reflection	99
5.3	Respect	104
	5.3.1 Limits and respect	107
5.4	Acceptance	110
5.5	Empathy	113
5.6	Sincerity and openness in contact	115
5.7	Confrontation	118
	5.7.1 Confrontation during supervision: an example from daily practice	121

References   125

About the author   127

Introduction

I am giving a series of classes on psychopathology to a group of about two dozen students and I am basing my seminars on one of the textbooks I have written. Sanne, an young woman in her early twenties, is one of the students. She says very little during the seminars, but follows what is being said with a critical expression on her face. In one of the last classes we are looking at the theme of transference and countertransference and towards the end I ask the students if they have any examples for me from their daily practice for a book I am writing about transference: this book. I see Sanne hesitate. 'Do you have an example for me?' I ask. 'I don't know,' Sanne says, 'I don't know if this is a good example.' 'Try us…!'
Sanne says that during the seminars she has recognized herself again and again in all the fears, neuroses, psychoses and in the various personality disorders. 'I've got that, I recognize that too. It's as if I've got them all.' She also says that as the seminars progressed, she has become more and more angry with me: that I could have the *nerve* to suggest that she's mad and has all sorts of neurotic traits, how *dare* I lay all these things on her… 'But why were you angry with me?' I ask in astonishment. 'Well, you wrote that book, didn't you?' says Sanne, full of righteous indignation.
It emerges that when Sanne was a teenager and probably even earlier, she was often told by her parents that she was a difficult and disturbed child. If she ever opposed her parents' wishes or spoke up for herself in any way, they would say: 'You're insane. You wait, you'll find out sooner or later how seriously disturbed you are. One day you'll see yourself as you really are!' and that was the end of that.
During the psychopathology seminars Sanne was confronted with herself, over and over again. It is as if her parents' voices echoed through my book, saying: 'One day you'll see yourself as you really are…' and she transferred the rage which was meant for her parents onto me, as though I personally had told her that she was 'insane', whilst it had in fact never entered my head.

10 Transference and Countertransference

Right from the time of the early socialization process in childhood through to the later process which takes us into adulthood, we are constantly developing patterns in our expectations of ourselves and of those around us. It is out of our experiences of ourselves in relation to others that we develop our sense of identity; these experiences lead to our conclusions, our convictions and our beliefs about ourselves and other people. Speaking very generally we might say that in our dealings with other people we often consciously, but also to a large extent unconsciously, transfer all sorts of feelings onto them: wishes, expectations, longings, fears and judgments. When we project the feelings which originate in the child in us, we call this transference.

> Jacob had a relatively secure childhood with parents who were kind and sympathetic; even as teenager he got on reasonably well with them both. At work Jacob is able to approach his supervisor with ease if there is anything troubling him and will always start out with the expectation that something will be done to help him; if everything has gone well, Jacob will be the first to say: 'Great day's work today!' Jacob's image of a supervisor is of a person who can be trusted, so he always starts by transferring onto his supervisor his own feeling of trust.
>
> Robert lost his father as a young child and there followed years of conflict with his stepfather, which escalated during his teenage years. He had the feeling that his mother never came to his defence and at seventeen he left home. It is for him a given that police, social workers and supervisors are not to be trusted. A personality test shows that he will have difficulty working under a boss. He works on the assumption that no supervisor will take him seriously and is already angry in anticipation of this. The consequence of his own mistrust is that right from the first moment Robert is on the defensive in his contact with a supervisor; his image is of a person who is not to be trusted, so that a supervisor will always evoke a feeling of suspicion in him.

Self-image

As a result of all our experiences, particularly but not exclusively those in early childhood, we piece together a picture of ourselves: our self-image.

Introduction

We learn to look at ourselves in a series of mirrors. Jacob has learned that he is a person who is worth listening to; Robert on the other hand always has the feeling that he has to defend himself.

Whilst we are forming our self-image, we are also developing our ideas about other people and how they see us: the other person will like me and that makes me happy, or the other person won't like me and I'm angry about it. We all have feelings, wishes, expectations and needs which we project onto other people in the course of our contact with them. The old feelings which do not always match the present situation we call transference feelings.

Transference

Transference feelings play a part in our non-volitional relationships with family, in our volitional relationships with friends, partner(s) and children and in work relationships with clients, customers, co-workers, supervisors and managers. In our daily contact with partners, children, friends and family, it can be useful to gain some insight into our own transference mechanisms: what of the other person's behaviour am I really seeing and what of myself am I projecting onto the other person? When we consider work situations in which we give guidance to other people and in which dependency plays some kind of role, it is not only useful but also advisable, and can maybe even be seen as a professional obligation, to gain some insight into our own transference mechanisms.

It is quite possible that when transference arises in a situation of inequality, some damage may be caused to the person who is in the dependent role; the client, the one in the 'subordinate' position, could be prevented by the transference issues of the more independent supervisor, care-practitioner or manager, from receiving the attention, recognition or acceptance that s/he needs and certainly deserves.

Getting to know our own sensitive spots, and more particularly learning about our own possibly hostile or malicious survival-strategies, can help us to be less harsh in our judgments of others; self-knowledge can greatly enrich our working relationships. Being able to admit to ourselves that we can have strange and sometimes malign thoughts about other people and that at times we only *just* have our behaviour under control, can give us the room to understand ourselves and others more fully.

The fifth edition

Some changes have been made in the lay-out of chapters and there are occasional small corrections and additions to the text.

An initial exploration of the terms transference and countertransference   1

In this opening chapter we will be making an initial acquaintance with the terms transference and countertransference; a closer examination will follow later in the book. We shall provide an indication of the kind of work situations and professional roles in which an understanding of these terms can be useful and we shall close with a summary of the content of further chapters.

The concepts *transference and countertransference* were originally developed by Sigmund Freud (1856-1939) to address the phenomenon within psychoanalysis – that is, within the classical therapeutic relationship – whereby old (child) feelings are projected or transferred by the client onto the therapist or in the case of countertransference, by the therapist onto the client.

Transference is a general term used to describe the way in which we bring feelings and expectations to bear upon other people. When the client does this we call it transference and when the (social care) practitioner does it we call it *counter*transference because this mostly arises as a reaction to the client's transference.

Transference: the client brings 'old', unconscious (child) feelings to bear on the care worker or other person upon whom s/he is to some degree dependent.
Countertransference: the care worker, in his or her position as authority-figure, brings old, unconscious (child) feelings to bear onto the client; this often occurs as a reaction to the behaviour of the client.

1.1 Projection and transference

Throughout this book we will make use of the term *projection*: that is to say, the bringing over or displacing of a certain image onto another person. It is possible that some confusion may arise over the meaning of the word projection when applied to transference, as opposed to its meaning when used to describe a defence mechanism, and there is a real difference here. In the context of transference we project an unconscious expectation about how the other person views us and we 'fill in' what the other sees in us and feels about us. Projection as a defence mechanism describes how we displace our own feelings unconsciously but directly onto the other person and how we then believe that this is what the other person is feeling. In many cases this takes the form of suppression: if we attribute our own unwanted or painful feelings to others, we do not need to feel them ourselves. The following examples serve to illustrate these two different forms of projection:

An example of projection as defence mechanism

Christina emerges from a conversation in her supervisor's office. Christina is a reliable worker who seldom calls in sick. When her supervisor asks her in for a chat, she is pleasantly surprised. As Christina leaves the office she bumps into Talita. 'What were you doing in there?' Talita asks. 'Well', says Christina, 'you know I was off ill for a few days…'. 'Oh, yes, and she had something to say about it I suppose!' Talita retorts. 'Not at all… at least she did – she wanted to ask me how I am. It was a very nice chat!' says Christina, slightly startled.

Here Talita projects onto Christina her own feelings, feelings which Christina does not recognize. If Talita had been called in by the supervisor, she would immediately have felt under attack and this feeling she attributes to Christina. She appears to be supporting Christina, whilst in fact she is simply expressing her own uncomfortable feelings.

In Talita's family you had to have a temperature of 100° before you were allowed to stay at home; there was never any question of 'just a day off to snuggle up on the sofa with Mummy', in fact no one ever paid very much attention to how she was feeling anyway. It has taken her years to allow herself to 'be ill' and although she can now manage it, taking time off work because of illness still gives her a lurking feeling of guilt and unease about being 'found out'. She would most definitely feel 'found out' if after a few days off sick she were called in for a chat with her supervisor! Without realizing it, Talita's unconscious feeling of guilt emerges in the form of anger which she projects onto Christina. She doesn't listen to Christina, she listens, unconsciously, to her own feelings and attributes them to Christina: this is the projection. She isn't angry with Christina, she is angry with the supervisor on Christina's behalf.

An example of transference

Talita is called in to see the supervisor. She has just been ill for a few days so she's bound to hear that she 'wasn't there, when we're already so short-staffed…'.
In the expectation that she will not 'be allowed' to be ill, as was the case in her childhood, Talita goes into the office with her hackles up. It's on the tip of her tongue to say: 'Okay, say it then, I didn't have double pneumonia and a temperature of 100° – yeah, and so what?'
Talita expects her supervisor to say that she shouldn't have stayed at home and in anticipation of this is already angry with the supervisor. Both feelings, the guilt and the anger, are old feelings which match her mother's behaviour then but do not fit with the supervisor's behaviour now: she is after all not angry with Talita in the slightest. What Talita feels and then projects onto her the supervisor are known as transference feelings.

1.2   Transference and countertransference

Originally the terms transference and countertransference did not receive particular attention in the psychoanalytical literature. It was only later that transference gradually began to take its place as a central concept within psychoanalysis and within the many new and rapidly-developing therapeutic forms and counselling models. What is certain is that Freud, in describing this mechanism, identified a very significant psychological phenomenon which is still of significant value to us.

Nowadays these concepts are used in a far more general context, and this is the basis upon which this book is written. All sorts of reactions can be traced to feelings from the past and all kinds of behaviour can be understood as the unconscious repetition of past forms of behaviour, particularly within relationships where dependency plays a part. These can include partner-relationships, parent-child relationships, counselling, supervisory and advisory situations, work relationships, leadership situations and coaching.

During a psychology class Lotte is irritated by the tutor's suggestion that our childhood experiences have an influence upon the way we bring up our own children. Lotte, who is fairly quick to go on the defensive anyway, says: 'I think that's ridiculous; I treat my children completely differently from how my parents treated me.' 'Can you give us an example of what you mean?' the tutor asks. 'Well', says Lotte, 'my mother was always really strict about everything. We had to be in for our tea every day at five on the dot. Even when the weather was fantastic and we wanted to play out longer, oh no, *we* had to go in whilst all our friends were allowed to stay out… Well I don't do that! We eat when we feel like it. Sometimes the children ask if we can eat early because they want to go off somewhere, and I say: No, no. We'll see when the time comes, I'm not going to be tied down to a fixed time…'.

The tutor asks with some bafflement what the difference is between this and what happened in Lotte's childhood. Very much as was the case then, the children now have no say in what time they eat. It's Lotte who decides, exactly as her mother always did. Lotte is not (yet) aware that her refusal to be 'tied down to a fixed time' originates in the feelings of an angry child and that although her behaviour appears to be the very opposite of her mother's, it does in fact amount to the same thing: just like her mother, she demands that her children adapt to her way of doing things and this is not a subject for discussion – as it wasn't then either. All this creates the same feeling of powerlessness in her own children that she herself experienced. Arising out of an old, angry feeling – because no one took account of her wishes – there is a voice in Lotte which keeps saying: 'I'm not going to fit in with what *you* want, so there!' So Lotte, in her turn, doesn't take account of her own children's wishes either, at least as far as mealtimes are concerned. This is an example, as we shall see later, of transference and countertransference: the projection of a child's feeling from the past within a situation which is characterized by dependency.

1.2.1 Recognizing similarities in a situation or a person

Transference feelings and issues can be evoked by similarities between a past and a present *situation*. The situation in the here-and-now carries features which are similar to the situation in, let's say, our family of origin.

Transference feelings can also be evoked by similarities in *persons*. In this sense we are dealing with someone who reminds us of a caregiver, a member of our family, a teacher or some other significant figure from our past. Transference feelings include a variety of *child-reactions* – expectations, wishes, longings, needs, judgments – which were originally connected to and evoked by parents or caregivers and can therefore be called 'old' feelings.

> *Unconscious transference feelings can disturb the therapeutic process. When made conscious they can make a significant and functional contribution to supervision, therapy, counselling or coaching sessions.*

Bart has been living in a reception centre for young people. Although he is himself still quite young, he is ready to start an independent life. Bart lost his father at a very early age and this has left him with a certain emotional vulnerability which he still carries. During his stay at the centre he has become attached to Ivar, his supervisor and mentor and, because he is afraid of losing his 'father' all over again, he is having great difficulty with the prospect of ending this contact. When Bart is encouraged by his mentor to speak openly about these feelings and to face and come to terms with his fear of loss, he can then begin the process of letting go of his dependence upon him. Transference feelings, when dealt with sensitively, can inform and deepen communication. In this case Bart gets to know himself better and can work consciously on the dependency he experiences in relation to particular male figures in his life who are of the age which his father would now have been. It could be that he was unable, as a young child having to deal with a grieving mother, to experience his own sadness fully. Taking the time to grieve now can help him to face his future in a more confident and adult way. In order to facilitate this process Ivar must be capable of maintaining a proper distance in his contact with Bart and must as a professional care practitioner be ready and willing to let go of his client. If Ivar were to need Bart's dependence upon him in order to maintain his own self-esteem or were to feel flattered by Bart's need, and if he were also unable to recognize these powerful feelings of dependency as transference, he would be unable to guide him properly through this necessary process of letting go. Here we would have an example of countertransference: Ivar would be likely to react in an immature and unprofessional way – in this case out of a childhood need of his own for attention – to the feelings of dependency which have been 'transferred' onto him by Bart.

Situations similar to the above example can occur not just in a therapeutic relationship but in a much wider variety of care settings. A client who lost his father at an early age or who for any other reason displays noticeably dependent behaviour towards a care practitioner can of course be found in any number of educational or care situations: in schools, in after school care, in centres for the disabled, in supervised housing projects, in detention centres or young offenders institutions, in home-care settings, in leadership situations and coaching sessions. Care workers, supervisors and their clients can be confronted with many similar issues of attachment and letting-go in the course of their daily work.

1.3 Professional guidance

This book is intended for people who offer professional guidance and support to others within the context of their personal development and who support them in finding solutions to the challenges which they encounter as part of this process. This definition includes not only managers, supervisors, care practitioners, social workers, counselors, teachers, child care and youth workers but doctors, health care practitioners, police and local authority officials, who can also be confronted in the course of their work with other people's transference issues and may find themselves manifesting the sort of less-than-professional behaviour that can be traced back to their own unresolved countertransference issues.

This book aims to include a broad and immediately recognizable range of situations in which practitioner and client, practitioner and supervisor, practitioner and colleague interact with one another and in which dependency, care and a certain level of personal closeness play a central role. Such situations arise on a daily basis within the care sector, in education, in counselling and coaching sessions and in management settings.

These situations could be said to fall roughly into three main categories: non-residential, semi-residential and fully-residential forms of care and support.

Non-residential is applied to (largely voluntary) situations in which people visit a practitioner or practitioners for a consultation or treatment and then go home again; this contact will not as a rule extend beyond a couple of hours. Therapy, counselling, coaching, supervision, medical and mental health care all fall into this category. One exception might be Video Home Training or a similar sort of intensive, home-based and often compulsory programme, but even here the contact is relatively short and clients remain in their own home.

The term *semi-residential* applies to facilities in which clients spend a part of of their time whilst (still) living in their own home, for example, organizations which offer intensive psychosocial help, special day care or after school care centres, but also more generally hospitals, community centres, regular day care centres for children, day care or training centres for people with a physical or mental disability, day care or activities for the elderly, schools of all kinds, sheltered workshops and similar organizations.

The term *residential* applies to facilities or institutions in which care, support and guidance is offered over an extended period of time to people who for that period live there; these include hospitals, nursing homes, care facilities for the elderly or those with a physical or an intellectual disability, psychiatric units, children's homes, young offenders institutions or secure units and prisons. It is in these settings, where an effort is often made to create a home atmosphere for what may be long-term residents, that practitioners are particularly likely to be met with their clients' relative dependency and with their memories of their own childhood homes, in the form of transference and countertransference.

Projection, whether conscious or unconscious, is a feature of every relationship we ever encounter, and therefore also of every professional care relationship: all the more reason for anyone who works professionally with people who experience themselves as dependent to become aware of the transference and countertransference issues inherent in these relationships.

Care practitioners can also, in their interaction with colleagues or supervisors, find themselves in a relatively dependent position and can in turn experience a tendency to project their own childhood feelings onto one of these 'authority figures'. It is clearly advisable for social care practitioners, coaches and counselors to be able to recognize transference in their clients and co-workers for the very reason that unconscious transference issues can work as a major hindrance and barrier to positive development. It is important that these issues are named and dealt with in a conscious way. The same applies to countertransference: if these issues and feelings are not made conscious they can form an obstruction to growth and change in client and care worker alike.

In order to gain insight into transference and countertransference mechanisms, as practitioners we need first of all to look critically at our own behaviour and our own intentions towards clients and colleagues – something which requires a certain amount of courage. It is quite possible that the process of becoming aware of what was until now unconscious transference may confront us with childhood feelings, not all of which will be comfortable or easy to accept. Self-awareness can evoke feelings of fear, not only of the confrontation with unconscious and painful emotions, but also of the sense of responsibility which inevitably comes with it.

This inner 'child' and the adult person are closely interwoven; extricating the child-feelings and responses can provide a challenging learning curve which is never easy and not always painless. It is, however, a professional condition of good practice that care practitioners are willing to enter into this process and to learn to reflect upon their own behaviour in order then to reflect upon:
- the behaviour shown by their clients
- their own relationship with their clients

Closeness and merging can often make fear seem to melt away, whilst the process of becoming aware of what is actually going on and the process of freeing oneself and letting go can be both painful and frightening; but it is this awareness which offers insight and creates space for reflection.

In this book every attempt has been made to explain the terms transference and countertransference in the clearest possible way, and to illustrate the concepts with examples from daily practice. These examples derive mainly from educational settings, supervision, coaching and therapy. Hopefully this book will contribute to an enquiry into the some of the feelings which may lie behind the decision to choose a career as a teacher, coach, counselor or social care worker and also into the way in which such feelings can be projected onto others in the course of this work.

In Chapter 2 the therapeutic terms transference and countertransference, as Freud developed them within psychoanalysis, are explained with the help of excerpts from Riekje Boswijk-Hummel's book *Liefde in Wonderland* and illustrated with examples from daily practice.
In Chapter 3 the process of transference and countertransference is explored from the perspective of the child within the adult, with reference to the theory behind Eric Berne's Transactional Analysis, the work of

Rita Kohnstam and Boswijk-Hummel and with the use of further examples from daily practice.

In Chapter 4 transference and countertransference is examined in the context of the practical situations in which it makes its appearance and is also looked at in relation to the concepts which characterize these situations, such as goal-directedness, interaction, communication techniques, semantics, distance, and closeness, and dependency.

In Chapter 5 transference and countertransference will be looked at in terms of the requirements and conditions which practitioners, coaches, counselors or supervisors must meet in the course of their daily work. The qualities and skills which contribute to the making of a responsive and productive social care practitioner or supervisor will be discussed in this chapter, with particular emphasis upon the role of transference and countertransference and the ways in which practitioners might deal with their own transference issues and the issues of those with whom they interact.

Transference and countertransference 2

As we have already mentioned in the introduction, transference is a concept which was developed by Sigmund Freud (1856-1939), the Viennese neurologist and founder of psychoanalysis. In this chapter the concept will be explored more closely with the help of psychoanalytical theory, the theory of Transactional Analysis and the work of Boswijk-Hummel on transference. The theory will be illustrated with examples from daily practice.

2.1 The psychoanalytical approach

Psychoanalysis takes as its starting point the idea that the human personality consists of three component parts, each of which exerts a continuous influence on the other two:

- *The Id.* The Id represents the instinctual nature: the reflexes and the basic emotions. The Id consists of:
  - the life drive: the instinct for survival, the need for pleasure, satiety and sexuality
  - the death drive: aggression, rage, the instinct to destroy

Both of these instincts are a source of energy, which Freud called libido. This energy is present in us all and it needs be discharged. The Id is the child in the individual, brimming with life force, spontaneity, impulses and longings. Children know instinctively what is pleasant and what is unpleasant. A gentle touch is pleasurable and is necessary to their growth; sprouts taste bitter and nasty. In the Id lie hidden the powerful feelings which we carry with us as children, the feelings which with time we learn to manage and to master with the help of the environment, our own learning experience and the other two emerging components of the personality: the Ego and the Superego. As children we want to have what we see, eat what we fancy and do what we feel like doing *right now*. If all goes well we learn, with the guidance of those around us, to control our impulses; in particular we learn to *defer gratification*. But the Id must be allowed to go on fulfilling its function: to be able to experience feelings and to trust those feelings is vitally important for us both as individuals and as professionals. If, as can sometimes happen, the Id becomes completely eclipsed by the Superego, it is a serious loss indeed because it means that we have to sacrifice our basic feeling experience.

The Id is as it were the 'gut feeling', the experiential knowing of whether things are pleasurable or not. Hidden in the Id are the often unconscious feeling-memories from childhood which can form a significant store of transference and countertransference issues.

- *The Superego*. The Superego is the part in us which we develop as a result of the influence of our caregivers, our environment, our community, our society and our culture; it takes the form of values, norms, habits, rules, moral sense and conscience: the 'shoulds'. The Superego is, we might say, the polar opposite of the Id: whilst the Id is focused on immediate gratification, the Superego strives to defer and to delay it. The Superego also tells us how we are or should be in the eyes of those around us, in other words it provides us with our self-image, also known as the 'ego-ideal'. Stored in the Superego are our ideals about ourselves, about others and about society. The Superego is the voice of our conscience which says: 'That's the right thing to do… if you do this you're a good person… don't do that… that's not allowed… you shouldn't have said that…'. It is the collection of moral and critical memories which is to be found in the Superego, the reservoir of transference and countertransference which feeds certain basic convictions and the feelings which go with them: it's okay for me to be as I am or it's not okay for me to be as I am. The Superego contains the prescriptive conscience and also the ability to experience feelings of shame and guilt.

- *The Ego*. The Ego or I is the most conscious and rational component of the personality and monitors the behaviour which we want other people to see. The Ego perceives what is happening in the environment and acts as a mediator between the Id and the Superego. The Ego channels feelings and emotions, defers gratification, carries out reality-checks, before making our behaviour visible and allowing us to present it to others. The Ego 'does deals' as it were, with the Superego and the Id, and after checking with the self-image and the environment, expresses in the form of behaviour the feelings, values and norms which it judges to be appropriate and acceptable in any given situation. With regard to transference and countertransference, the Ego, with its rational knowing, has the function of making us aware of the way in which 'old' feelings from the Id and the Superego can influence and sometimes disturb our relationships in the here-and-now.

These three components combine to form our personality. Transference occurs when the Ego is not alert enough or strong enough to negotiate effectively between the Superego and the Id. Feelings, which objectively speaking are not appropriate to the situation, are projected from either the Id or the Superego onto another person. This is almost always connected to the intensity of the feelings which have been evoked either by the person or by the nature of situation; as a result the Ego is temporarily swamped and is unable to perform its monitoring function. Later, however, when the intensity of the emotion has subsided, the Ego can once more be called upon to assess and adjust the behaviour in question.
Psychoanalytical theory is often typified as a conflict theory, because the three components are constantly vying for influence and from time to time can be at serious loggerheads with each other. All three, simultaneously but not in equal measure, have a real effect on practical actions and transactions. What we often see in the case of personality disorders is that the Ego function is disturbed: the person in question is not able to mediate properly between the three parts and the Ego loses its hold on things.
The following short examples illustrate the functioning of the three components; they are taken from an educational setting but can easily be applied to other situations.

> You are following a class at college and you disagree with something the lecturer is saying. Here are a few possible reactions you might have, some of which reveal the positive and others the negative convictions you may hold:
> - You want to say that you disagree. You think: Can I do this, can I contradict the lecturer? Can I get away with it? What are the rules here? (Superego)
> - You think: the lecturer won't listen to what I have to say, she'll think I'm stupid… (Superego: ego ideal 'I don't meet the standards here…')
> - You think spontaneously: Of course I can say what I think, this is my opinion. I feel free to say whatever I like. (Id)
> - You start to feel angry and you think: Who does she think she is? I can think what I like even if no one else agrees with me, why should I keep my mouth shut? (Id)
> - You say what you think because you have the courage of your convictions. (Ego, on the basis of positive Id and Superego content: the conviction that you will be heard)
> - You don't say what you think because you don't dare to. (Ego, on the basis of negative Id and Superego content: the conviction that you will not be heard)
> - You say what you think (Ego), but because you already believe (Superego) that nobody will agree with you, you say it in such an aggressive way (Id) that you soon have a conflict on your hands.
> - You know that you can tend to adopt an aggressive tone if you disagree with something (co-operation between Id and Superego). You take a deep breath and state your opinion calmly. (Ego)

The Id works on the *pleasure principal*, the Superego works on the *moral or idealization principal* and the Ego on the *reality principal*. Many of our childhood experiences are unconscious and remain stored as content in the Id or the Superego and play a positive, a neutral or a negative role in the way we think, feel and act in the present moment. When unconscious experiences start to have an adverse effect on our lives, we can call upon the Ego to make these memories conscious in a number of ways: by listening to and thinking about feedback from others, by means of self-reflection, or by entering into the process of self-discovery involved in a therapeutic, counselling or coaching relationship. As soon as unconscious feelings stored in the Id and the Superego are made conscious, the client or the practitioner can start to work with and upon them.

We are all influenced to some degree in our current thinking, feeling and actions by earlier, and more particularly, very early experiences. If these experiences were of warmth, security and respect, we shall always have an easily-accessible well of rich resources to draw upon. It is altogether trickier if the well is full of insecurity, fear or sadness; it will then cost a great deal of effort and energy to be able trust other people, enter into relationships or work together successfully with others in the here-and-now.

According to Freud, the feelings which are discussed in this book in terms of transference and countertransference are projected from the unconscious onto others; they are dormant feelings from the past which are stored in a part of the Id or the Superego. As well as this, thoughts and actions in the mediating Ego can also exert an unconscious influence on the effects of our behaviour. In the following example it almost painful to witness how Paul compensates for his own shortcomings by trying very hard to get everything right for himself and for the people around him, but in doing this unconsciously ignores their boundaries. Because in the past his boundaries and needs were neither seen nor acknowledged, he fails in his turn to acknowledge other people's boundaries in his eager attempts to make everything 'okay'. He projects onto others the need: 'See me and hear me', but quite forgets to listen to them, whilst all this is quite the opposite of what he consciously intends.

> Paul comes from a family where there was plenty of money but very little warmth: on the feast of St. Nicholas* there were always lots of lavish and expensive presents but there were very few verses and as a rule the atmosphere was not very happy.
> *translator's note: the festival of St. Nicholas or Sinterklaas is celebrated in the Netherlands on 5th December with the exchanging of gifts; it is the custom to accompany a gift with a personal and usually humorous rhyming verse, written by the giver.

> If someone did happen to write a verse it was usually critical, malicious and unfunny. Since leaving home Paul has for many years celebrated St. Nicholas with friends. He buys small but carefully chosen gifts for everybody which he accompanies with certainly humorous, but also interminable verses; this means that these evenings are endlessly long and also that the less gifted poets of the company start to feel more and more uncomfortable as the night wears on. In the end a good friend of Paul's tries to point out to him tactfully that a bit less might go a long way. The realization gradually dawns on Paul that what he has actually been doing is trying to compensate for what he himself missed: long and happy hours in each other's company with lots and lots of amusing and affectionate verses. From the place of his Superego he wants to be the ideal gift-giver and writer-of-verses: with thoughtful little presents and carefully-worded poems. But his Ego had lost sight of the people around him who have had to sit through the last few poems stifling yawns and fighting off sleep. Paul, who as a child had so longed to be seen, had temporarily lost sight of what was going on around him. And... he *was* seen and heard by his friends, but at the end of the evening only out of politeness.

Following the explanation of the terms transference and countertransference as they are defined within psychoanalysis, we shall look at these concepts from the more general point of view of the personal supervisor, using illustrations from daily practice.

2.2 Transference

The phenomenon of transference was first observed by Freud in the course of his work with the clients who came to him for psychoanalysis. It began to strike him that clients were projecting onto him, in his capacity as therapist, emotions from their childhood years which would then have been directed at their parents, caregivers or other significant figures. During therapy it is as if clients attribute qualities and characteristics to the therapist which actually belong to figures from the past. These figures may have been dearly loved or bitterly hated, can have withheld their love or been objects of fear, but in the intimacy of therapy early feelings of whatever sort start to re-emerge. Childhood feelings are evoked anew and often re-experienced in all their intensity in the therapy room. Within analytical therapy the reliving of feelings is a prerequisite for being able to come to terms with experiences from the past which are blocking personal development in the present. If old feelings of rage or fear or extreme dependency are deeply buried and unfulfilled needs are not acknowledged, they are likely to cause problems of all kinds within intimate relationships in later life.

Whilst it is true to say that transference feelings by their nature or intensity do not match the present situation, they can certainly arise out of it. This happens in a therapeutic setting but it can also happen within a more general care-context or within any relationship in which dependency is a feature. Indeed it is the current relationship or situation which actually evokes (or 'triggers') the transference feelings which are connected to an unconscious stream of early childhood responses stored in the Id and the Superego. Transference feelings in their turn largely determine the nature of dependent relationships in the present.

Freud discovered that many of the difficult feelings which were projected onto him by his patients were not in fact intended for him. Experience also taught him that when these feelings could be recognized and elucidated, they could be used as an effective therapeutic tool, perhaps indeed the most effective he had yet come across. This requires of course from therapists and practitioners that they are able to recognize the transferred feelings in the client for what they are and that they are also conscious of their own possible transference and countertransference issues. They must be willing to investigate and recognize their own feelings and behaviour because their own reactions to the client's transference will have a significant influence on the outcome of the therapy, working relationship or contact and may even determine its degree of success.

> Nick is angry with his therapist. All that 'talk' is a waste of time, he says, and what is more the therapist refuses to give him any proper advice. 'Why don't you just tell me what I should do? You've followed years of study for this, you must have some idea of what the problem is and therefore what

the solution might be!' Nick's anger originates in the fact that he had very strict parents who insisted upon obedience, compliance and academic success without offering him any emotional support at all. They bought him lots of expensive things, but never anything he really wanted. At mealtimes the conversation was always about money and study, never about longings or fears, sexuality or bad dreams. Because there is attention for it in his therapy, Nick begins to experience ever more intensely the pain of the emotional abandonment he experienced as a child. He wants the therapist to take the pain away – to find a 'solution' to the 'problem' for him. He is angry with his therapist because he experiences the difficult childhood feelings of helplessness in his presence. He is angry with his parents who ignored his emotional needs and he displaces this anger onto his therapist: this is the transference.

On the one hand he is angry because his parents used to decide everything for him and on the other hand this has also made him dependent. Now Nick wants the therapist to tell him what he feels and what he should be feeling: that is his expectation. Acting out of his early feelings of helplessness, when he had no freedom to make his own choices, Nick now expects that someone else, in this case the therapist, will tell him what to do: transference. What makes this so complicated is that it is not what he really needs – it won't help him and would just be a continuation of what always happened – and yet this is what Nick wants. What is more, he can accuse the therapist of being unprofessional because he doesn't feel that he has been helped.

What he knows about is being controlled from outside. If the therapist complies with his wishes and tells Nick what he should do, this will in the end not serve him; it will only confirm him in his dependency rather than stimulate him in his own potential for self-direction.

2.3 Resistance

The anger which this client experiences can also be called 'resistance', a concept which was also developed by Freud. Change is often painful and feeling like a small child can evoke feelings of fear and insecurity. None of us wants to feel pain – even if the 're-experiencing of old feelings' is

a prerequisite for change. Change is scary and feels unsafe and evokes a fear of loss of identity. Sometimes we do not recognize ourselves any more, or we fear that other people may not recognize us.
We resist unwelcome feelings and fearful uncertainty; we know who we were and what we had – or didn't have – but we do not know where this new situation and these new feelings will lead us.
Resistance can take many forms: anger, clinging, protracted silences, 'forgetting' appointments: it is Freud's term for unconscious opposition to change. Care practitioners need to know and understand resistance, to recognize it and to approach it in their clients with respect. Resistance can only be relinquished if the client is able to feel it and see it for what it is and this means that the practitioner must also be able to recognize it in order to guide the client. Only then will it be possible for the client to acknowledge and then begin to let go of these difficult feelings.

> Justina is eight years old. She has been given an emergency placement by the child protection service in a crisis centre awaiting a court order which will decide her immediate future. Justina has been wandering the streets until late in the evening, her mother lies in bed all day and there are fears that Justina is being abused by her stepfather. The staff at school have been concerned about her for some time because she often comes late and looks neglected. Justina is now safe. She arrives at school on time and looks well-cared for. Now that she feels safe and no longer needs to worry about her mother or to live in fear of her stepfather, the panic that she has had to suppress all these months comes to the surface. There is only chaos and loneliness inside her. She has no idea where to turn and she expresses her panic by hurling abuse at the care workers: it's all their fault that she's stuck here and she wants to go home.
> Her carers understand why Justina is so angry. They think she is a very brave little girl and what they really would like to do is to tuck her up in bed with a big hug and read her a story. Just at the moment this would be too intimidating for Justina. She is looked after with kindness but her carers keep their distance. It is fine for her to be angry, within certain limits. Her resistance, her feelings of powerlessness, panic and confusion are treated with respect.

A condition for good practice in care work and supervision is that the practitioner recognizes resistance in the client for what it is, understands it and can then put the client's behaviour into words in an accessible and comprehensible way: 'You would really like me to solve this for you, and I would like to be able to, only…'.

To return to Nick's case: 'Acting out of the helplessness of his early childhood, when he was not given the freedom to make choices for himself, Nick expects the therapist to tell him what to do.' This is a difficult moment for the therapist because he wants to offer his support, but what he is asking for will not help Nick to become independent. The therapist cannot offer direct help by prescribing solutions and instead must find a way of making it clear to his client that his expectations have to do with 'old' feelings and that he can only deal with his present problems if he gains some insight into this longing and this process.

> Kirsty is in her early twenties and has supervision as part of her teacher training. In the introductory session she talks about herself, her childhood, her parents, her career choice, her teaching practice, her boyfriend. The supervisor asks Kirsty what her personal objectives are at the moment. Important goals for Kirsty are: learning to deal with criticism, developing her self-identity and learning to act out of a sense of authority.
>
> Soon after Kirsty was born her father left her mother for another woman. Kirsty has the feeling that she was never unconditionally loved and accepted by her mother; she always felt that she had to compensate for something: her father's departure. Kirsty's mother had lost her own mother when she was thirteen and she had experienced this loss as a terrible abandonment. On top of this, her abandonment by her husband so soon after Kirsty's birth, was more than she could bear. Possibly acting out of an unconscious fear of losing Kirsty as well, her mother kept her under tight control and set her daughter impossibly high standards; Kirsty did her best but it was never good enough and she felt that she was constantly under surveillance. Being checked on all the time gave her the feeling that she was clearly not to be trusted and was really not capable of much, and what is more that she was not wanted and that she constantly needed to justify her existence. Her potential for self-acceptance and self-development was blocked because all her energy went into proving that she could

be trusted; she was never allowed just 'to be'. At seventeen, after years of conflict, Kirsty left home.

Her female supervisor sees a delightful, slightly fragile-looking young woman sitting opposite her. What a tragedy, she thinks, that this daughter and this mother have never been able to enjoy one other. She feels the impulse to take this young girl in her arms and tell her that she's beautiful just as she is, but life isn't like that and neither is supervision, so they talk about study, teaching practice and personal objectives.

During their third session Kirsty suddenly announces that she is thinking of looking for another supervisor. Her supervisor is shocked but keeps this to herself, saying instead that she would find that a pity and suggesting that they try to work out together why Kirsty is not happy with the supervision. What emerges is that Kirsty feels that her supervisor is not giving her enough confirmation: 'You listen to me, you talk things over with me, but you never tell me whether I'm getting things right or not. I feel as if you just leave me to sink or swim.'

Kirsty is angry with the mother who dictated constantly how she should behave, yet at the same time, unconsciously, she expects this same treatment from her supervisor: 'Tell me what I'm doing right and what I'm doing wrong!' Going in search of her own feelings and wishes evokes panic in her; she feels she *has* to swim or she will sink, so she is unable to enjoy the process of 'swimming' for its own sake. She doesn't want to feel the uncertainty of it: we can call this resistance. She is willing to try and find herself but she doesn't want to experience that feeling of despair, it is too painful and too confronting; she would sooner walk away from it- and end the supervision.

In this third session Kirsty's emotional conflict is addressed; if other people do not give her approval and do not say: 'That's right' or 'That's how you should do it', she feels worthless and walks away with an angry feeling: 'Okay, I suppose I'll have to work it out for myself then!' Confirmation and approval give her short-lived relief, but because it has to come from others and not from herself she has to keep on looking for this approval time after time. Not being approved of evokes feelings of panic and anger.

And yet… staying with that feeling of doubt and despair is the only way for her to learn who she is and what she wants. During her supervision Kirsty's doubts are taken seriously by her supervisor and this enables

> Kirsty to start taking her doubts and herself seriously too: she starts to allow herself to have doubts and to make mistakes. In this way Kirsty and her supervisor can embark upon a journey of discovery together; Kirsty starts to accept that doubt and uncertainty are for the moment part of her identity and she carries on with the supervision.

2.4 Countertransference

Countertransference is the transference from practitioner onto the client, and it usually occurs as a reaction to the client's transference. If the practitioner in the former example of transference and resistance were to concur with the expectations – the transference – of the client, if she were in other words to 'mother' her and to control her, she would simply repeat what the client's mother did and nothing in the client's world would change. When the reaction of the practitioner comes from her old, unassimilated feelings, then we call this *countertransference*.

Here we have an example of countertransference, which follows the line of the two previous practical examples.

> A client who shows symptoms of overstress, who works constantly and is in despair because he has started forgetting things, who is the son of extremely demanding parents and who's own marriage is falling apart, says to his therapist: 'Why don't you just tell me what I should do? You've followed years of study for this… you must have some idea what the problem is and therefore what the solution might be…'. The therapist is disturbed or hurt by the fact that the client, who is himself highly educated, might have doubts about his professional ability. Contrary to his usual practice and way of working, he gives his client some practical advice about taking it a bit easier at work. He also gives him a few concrete tips to help him to salvage his failing marriage. He ignores the client's anger and despair, skirts round the palpable area of tension and complies with the client's request.

> He doesn't pinpoint the source of the anger (powerlessness in the face of 'new' and unfamiliar feelings), neither does he question the client's explicitly stated expectation that the therapist should define the problem and find a solution (whilst the client is himself angry with his parents for always telling him what he should feel and do), nor does he ask the client what the deeper intention might be behind the words: 'You've followed years of study for this' (whilst the client is so furious about the exacting educational demands which his parents made upon him).
>
> He avoids the client's resistance by not mentioning it and makes no connection between his anger with his controlling parents and his paradoxical wish to be controlled by the therapist. By doing this he leaves out an important piece of the process because he is motivated by his wish to comply with the client's wish for concrete advice and is driven by his own need to be held in professional esteem: this is his countertransference.
>
> This need or countertransference issue arises out of the therapist's own painful experience. He was the only one of his large family to enjoy a university education after leaving school. His father always said: 'He'd better not start fancying himself just because he's got letters after his name. He mustn't go thinking that he's better than the rest of us… in fact there'll come a day when he'll realize he doesn't amount to much…'.
>
> Confronted now with an older man who speaks in the same denigrating tones as his father once did, the therapist is thrown off balance and tries as it were to arm himself – with inappropriate defence mechanisms – against his own fear of failure. He feels very uncomfortable in the situation and reacts out of his own transference to the transference of his client: countertransference.

According to Freud, countertransference is the (unconscious) feeling which arises in the therapist or care-practitioner as a reaction to the client's projected feelings – in the above example the uneasy feeling which the therapist has of being seen as a failure and of not being respected. The client touches a sensitive spot in the therapist and makes him feel powerless. If this therapist had been less susceptible and less intimidated by his client's social and educational standing, he would have been able to maintain the necessary distance to help clarify the client's feelings to and with him. If his countertransference had been consciously available to him, the therapist could have been touched by his client's remarks, but would not have allowed himself to be side-tracked by them.

Unconscious countertransference can have an adverse effect upon the neutral position which a therapist needs to maintain.

In the last example, the therapist has temporarily lost his professional perspective. He reacts out of his own hurt feelings instead of keeping his focus on what this (difficult and demanding) client needs: his own vulnerability clouds his vision and he loses sight of what is driving the client's behaviour.

- An unconscious Superego drives the client to keep working, to keep meeting the demands of others.
- An unconscious Id is where the rage and the despair come from: nothing is ever good enough.
- The behaviour that the client shows to the world (the Ego): 'I demand that you advise and rescue me now and if you don't do that quickly then as far as I'm concerned you don't amount to much, however many letters you have after your name'.

By behaving in this way, the client is digging himself into a hole and making sure that he will not be able to change his current situation; it is the therapist's task to reflect this behaviour back to the client and to help him to recognize it.

Countertransference which the practitioner is aware of need not present any problem provided that s/he is able to manage it properly.

If the therapist had been aware of his own countertransference he would still have been affected by his client's remark and at the same time he would have realized that this man happens to *remind* him of his father but that he *is not* his father. Of course the client is conveying something very specific with his remark: people are only worthwhile if they are highly educated. What does this say about this overworked, overstressed man and the way he sees himself as a person? This is the question which the therapist might need to address.

If practitioners feels hurt by a client's remarks, this can provide a useful indication of which way the conversation may need to go. What does the client mean by this remark, both in relation to the practitioner and to himself? What the client in the previous example needs is to gain insight into the fact that the attitude he takes towards himself and other people is the very same controlling, demanding attitude that his parents took towards him and is also the very attitude which makes him so angry. In the case study he is controlling and demanding towards his therapist, but sooner or later he is bound to behave in this aggrieved and demanding way in his contact with others in his work and in his private life. This attitude is not conducive to a good working relationship; on the contrary, it is likely to evoke defensive reactions in other people. The therapist could for instance, tell the client how his behaviour makes him feel and could then ask him if it is his intention to make him feel like this. It is possible that the client will then recognize in the therapist's mirroring the feelings that he had as a child and will learn to reflect upon his own behaviour.

2.5 Some general comments about transference and countertransference

Wherever dependency and intimacy feature in a relationship, transference and countertransference will come into play. Transference and countertransference issues are always with us; we all carry are own archive around with us in which our old feelings and (unfulfilled) wishes are filed: a storehouse of precious and not-so-precious memories which play both a conscious and an unconscious role in our behaviour. The precious memories provide us with a source of effortless and trouble-free transference: we can draw on these reserves of trust, warmth, humour and intimacy whenever we like. The not-so-precious memories provide a source of knowledge and life-experience: both are of great benefit in social professions. However, care and conscious awareness are of the essence here because transference which comes from not-so-precious memories can get in the way of fruitful interaction.

Students sometimes get a little weary of me when I ask them questions about what might lie behind their actions: 'You always think that everything has to have a *reason.*' Some students say: 'But this is just the way I am,' or 'I've been doing this for years and nobody's ever said anything about it before,' or 'Everybody's like that sometimes,' if I give them feedback about their attitude or their behaviour. Yet whether we want to see it or not – and as a social care practitioner, educator, supervisor, manager, counselor or coach, we *do need* to see it – all behaviour has an intention behind it, all behaviour has an effect upon other people and some of the reactions which are evoked by behaviour we call transference and countertransference, most particularly where these reactions occur within a relationship of dependency or social care.

A few general remarks:
- Transference feelings which are projected onto a practitioner are of course specific to the client, but in a way they can be seen in a more general perspective, in that almost all clients are, certainly at first, likely to adopt a dependent position in relation to the practitioner; it is the degree of, say, helplessness or anger which varies from client to client.
- Countertransference feelings which are projected by the practitioner onto the client are specific to the practitioner, but can also be seen in more general terms. All practitioners will occasionally feel discouraged by a client's helplessness, but just how much irritation this evokes, or to what extent it makes them behave in a patronizing or directive way, will again depend upon the individual practitioner.
- Whilst transference and countertransference feelings are unique in each case, the same feelings do tend to recur. Transference is particular to each relationship but carries features which are common to all dependent relationships.
- Whilst every relationship is unique, a client can evoke the same kinds of feelings in different people: co-workers, supervisors, and practitioners. Some clients may use an irritating, nagging voice or an aggressive tone, or they may come across as arrogant and demanding. This behaviour will be discernible to every practitioner, but the role which the behaviour plays in the client/practitioner relationship and the way in which the practitioner deals with it will be different in every relationship.
- Although each relationship is unique, one particular therapist, practitioner, supervisor or educator can evoke the same feelings in different clients. One practitioner gives an impression of authority, another a feeling of warmth. These impressions will be perceived by every client but the influence they have upon the contact will vary in every case.

The range of feelings which we are able to project is related to the whole scale of feelings which we experience: from fury to longing, from sensuality to aversion, from sympathy to indifference, from irritation to tenderness. The way in which a client reacts to the individuality and the conduct of the practitioner, and how a practitioner reacts to the individuality and conduct of the client, will define the nature and progress of the care-relationship.

A practical illustration of the above points:

> Kelly is a warm, reasonably self-assured manager who can assess and deal with situations with considerable natural authority. She has just joined an organization which has recently endured a long period of changes in management: a manager with burn-out, a manager who left to have a baby, a couple of managers who didn't do their job very well. Kelly accepted this job knowing that, after such a period of relative chaos, she might meet with some understandable resistance in her staff. Just as in a family situation, it is often the case that the emotions which are meant for the non-functioning parent or manager are evoked by or indeed projected upon the one who finally offers the longed-for security and structure; it is as if only now is it safe enough to express the emotions which belong to the past and were in fact intended for someone else.
>
> As one of her first tasks Kelly sets about reinstating a programme of staff assessments. She makes it clear that she is open to feedback but she also challenges and confronts her staff and they have to get used to the fact that close attention is once again being paid to what they do. A small number of them find her unpleasantly authoritarian: 'Who does she think she is, walking in here after all these years of bad management and thinking that she can have things all her own way?' The majority of the workers find her presence a relief because they feel 'seen' once more; they find her pleasantly authoritative. Now the workers who think she is authoritarian tend to be the ones who don't have a great deal of self-confidence; they find it difficult to voice their opinion, even if Kelly asks for it, because they think that their views will carry no weight. Some of them don't want to be seen; it makes them feel that they are being checked up on and because some aspects of their work in fact leave a lot to be desired – if left to them-

> selves they tend not to work as hard as they could, for instance – they don't welcome this one bit. The members of her staff who don't see Kelly as a threat are those who generally speaking are able to say what they think and who have been able to function in an independent and reasonably satisfying way during the last difficult period.
> As well as clearly being a woman whom it is impossible to ignore, Kelly is also an authority figure upon whom the workers can project their own feelings of satisfaction and confidence, or lack thereof.

The way in which we view other people's behaviour is coloured by our own self-image. Research shows that people with a positive, well-adjusted self-image have, from their position of self-confidence, a more realistic perception of other people's behaviour than those with a negative or over-positive self-image. Those of us with too little self-confidence, and those who try to shout down their negative self-image, have the tendency to misjudge other people's conduct and intentions as either more negative or more positive then they in fact are. Self-image is an important breeding ground for projections and its positive or negative colour will affect the way in which other people and their intentions are judged. In the light of this it would seem obvious that social care practitioners need to be familiar with the 'colour range' of their own projections, at least in the broadest sense, in order to be able recognize potentially unproductive countertransference.

2.6 Transformation processes and transference

In her book about transference and countertransference *Liefde in Wonderland* (1997) Riekje Boswijk-Hummel describes transference as a process, one which unfolds within a (care) relationship. Some clients will experience within this relationship the kind of respect from another person which they have never encountered before: someone who really tries to see them as they are, who gets to know them in their deeper thoughts and feelings and who meets a need which may have been lying dormant for years. It can feel as though the client has found the 'ideal' father or mother and can then project their inner fantasies upon the practitioner: 'This person understands me, this person is going to "rescue" me'. These projections are almost always unconscious, although many who have had experience of such conversations will recall certain comforting thoughts: 'It felt like a warm bath', or the relief of: 'At last something was really going to happen, it was all going to come right', as well as the stab of rage and rejection you felt the day your counselor forgot the name of your partner or your child. All this stems from the expectation that the practitioner is totally trustworthy, remembers everything you ever said and is completely emotionally stable: in other words is the Ideal Parent.

The progress of a care relationship could look something like this:
- The client feels alone, misunderstood and unhappy.
- Arising out of these feelings the client has a need for something to hold onto and a need to be shown the way.
- The client carries an ideal image of the one who would be able to offer this; compare this with fantasies about the 'ideal' partner.
- Within the contact with the practitioner the client feels understood, safe and secure, often for the first time.
- This puts the practitioner in the position of *the* person on whom the client can project ideal images and expectations: *transference*.
- These transference issues then form part of the process within the relationship and the practitioner has a duty to see, recognize and work with these issues.
- After a period of relative dependency, the client will need to let go of this. Together the practitioner and the client work towards bringing the relationship to a close.

According to Boswijk-Hummel there are a number of possible pitfalls in this process:
- Countertransference, in the form of the (unconscious) need to be 'put on a pedestal' or to be the 'knight in shining armour', can cause an inequality in the practitioner/client relationship which will render it dysfunctional. The practitioner stays in the role of the guru, parent or authority figure because this is where *s/he* feels most comfortable.
- The practitioner turns out to be an ordinary person after all and falls – in the eyes of the client – from the pedestal with a crash. If this transference, this idealization, is not addressed, the client is likely to go away with the idea that s/he must go on looking for the 'ideal helper'

– were such a thing to exist. The client remains stuck in the old expectation and continues to search for the ideal parent who is nowhere to be found. As long as the client goes on doing this, s/he will have great difficulty in becoming a mature adult.

During the unfolding process between practitioner and client it is the practitioner in particular who must stay alert to what is emerging and at which stage in the relationship it emerges. Temporary relationships, of a non-residential kind, usually have three distinct phases – an initial, exploratory phase, a central phase of working together and a rounding off phase of letting go and ending.

In her book 'Kleine Ontwikkelingspsychologie' (1993) Rita Kohnstamm describes how children, on their way towards adulthood, pass through the three phases: *dependency, attachment and independence*. At first children are dependent upon the people who happen to be their parents or caregivers; they have no choice in the matter. Then comes the phase in which children start to form attachments. Positive attachment has much more to do with the quality of the attention which is given to growing children than the quantity: their parents' responsiveness and the ability to react to their signals is more important than 'being there all the time'; children form the best attachments to parents who when present are responsive and emotionally available. An attached child will in the end attain independence whereas children who are unable to form attachments, because their parents are unavailable or cannot be trusted, will experience much more difficulty in becoming independent later on. Such a child may grow into an unstable, dependent adult, or one who exhibits a fierce but false form of independence.

A care process can follow a similar course: practitioner and client enter into a form of contact which connects them with one another for a certain period of time. Clients are seldom able to choose their counselors or supervisors and at first clients feel to a large extent dependent upon the care and attention which are being offered. If they feel understood they will be willing to develop within the relationship: responsiveness on the part of the practitioner encourages in the client the willingness to grow. A functional form of attachment will develop between the client and the practitioner and over time the (therapeutic) relationship will gradually become more equal and the participants will move into a phase in which they can work together. When the client reaches emotional independence it will mean that the time has come to end the relationship and there will be a phase in which it is slowly brought to a close. The contact is then ended and goodbyes can be said.

Transference and countertransference seen from the child-position

Looking at transference and countertransference from the perspective of Transactional Analysis

Both transference and countertransference have their source in the child within the adult person – within the client, the supervisor, coach or social care practitioner. This child does not suddenly appear, neither at birth nor at any particular point thereafter. The child within the adult is not a constant factor; its development is based upon the interaction between child's own disposition and the environment. Children will of course always retain elements of their own intrinsic nature but they will to a large extent be formed by the way in which other people show them who they are, how they should be and who they are expected to become. As adults we carry the image of the child within us, not so much the child we were but the child as others saw us and mirrored back to ourselves: the child as we were seen and experienced by those who brought us up, our teachers and those in our immediate environment. The child we wanted to be, the child we definitely did *not* want to be, the child we were, the child others wanted us to be- as adults we carry all these facets within us without necessarily being conscious of them.

3.1 'To be or not to be'

Young babies do not yet have any conscious expectations about the way in which their caregivers behave; they only begin to become aware of their own existence from the age of about six months. Little by little and in constant interaction with their environment, babies begin to develop an image of themselves and at the same time to develop expectations about the adults around them. These expectations will develop in direct relationship to the kind of behaviour which their caregivers display.

Responsive caregivers, who are aware of and appreciate a child's unfolding possibilities, will be able to respect their children's integrity and not damage them, because their children will be seen as being on a journey of discovery, in need of respectfully given boundaries but not to be punished for this urgent need to explore. Children who are treated in this way will develop the feeling that they have the right to exist, that they can take the room they need to develop, that they possess a degree of self-mastery and can exert an influence on their environment.

The child experiences the unconditional right to 'be' as s/he is.

Caregivers who are unable to appreciate the unfolding possibilities of growing children will be more likely to experience them as troublesome and manipulative than as explorative. There may be a tendency to punish the child more frequently. With this goes the possibility that such children may become wary of adults and may see themselves as a nuisance and a burden. This idea of being seen as a burden by their caregivers (and later by themselves) does not stop here; they attribute this opinion to other adults as well. A possible reaction to this is that children become over-adaptive in their attempt to be unobtrusive; alternatively they may develop into children who invest most of their energy in being manipulative and in testing boundaries – this way they will at least be 'seen'. If children are not encouraged or rewarded in their normal attempts to adapt, they will never be able to learn what is expected of them and will soon no longer see the point of trying to adjust their behaviour to meet the wishes of others.

> Lena is an inquisitive child who asks lots of questions. Possibly because she does not always know the answers, her mother tells Lena that she must be stupid if she needs to keep asking questions all the time. Lena does not stop asking questions but she does internalize the conviction that she is stupid. Having completed a vocational training with excellent results, she is to her own astonishment accepted for a university course. When she enters therapy to help her deal with her own rejection of herself as stupid, her mother says that she always knew there was something wrong with her with all those endless questions of hers…

The child is not allowed to 'be'; his/her existence is conditional.

Children who are not seen as they are may develop into guarded, cautious adults who are dogged by the fear of failure. On the other hand children who are never seen may become an all-too-visible scourge for their immediate environment and for society as a whole.

3.1.1   Self-awareness

The basis for self-awareness is laid down in early childhood, usually before the fourth year. From the age of about six months babies will become increasingly aware of their surroundings; as they start to develop the ability to create a mental image of themselves as separate from their environment, they will also be learning to walk. Their drive to explore the world will be at its height. They learn their first words, including 'yes' and even more importantly, 'no'. These experiences have a major and far-reaching emotional impact on small children. Because they are now capable of making independent contact with those around them, their social context will begin to transform.

Whilst up to now he has mostly had to eat the food that was presented to him, the baby now begins to discover his own tastes and starts to indicate what and when he wants to eat. He starts to explore his own boundaries. Because he is beginning to discover that he is 'somebody', he will now want to assert this, regardless of the situation. If he sees a toy he fancies, he takes or grabs it. He knocks other children over if they get in his way because he cannot yet put himself in the other person's shoes. He may hit adults or other children, not because he thinks that it will hurt them, but because it makes a funny noise or creates an unexpected effect: it's exciting! He will kiss children he has never met before simply because he is happy to see other children. If the child has to go with his parents but would rather stay where he is, or would like to go whilst his parents prefer to stay, he will now protest at the top of his lungs instead of being the model of compliance he was until just a short time ago. He is on a journey of self-discovery but is not yet in command of himself nor can he foresee the consequences of his actions. With so many new things happening in his young life he tires easily, but between naps he seems to have boundless energy.

This phase of development makes large demands upon a child's caregivers, particularly upon their patience and their capacity for responsiveness. It appears as if children of this age are only too aware of what they are doing: they will challenge you with a look whilst repeating *precisely* what you have just said they are not to do. But the fact is that toddlers do not yet know what 'forbidden' means, nor what might cause harm to other people or to themselves: they do not yet have a conscience. This develops gradually and under the influence of other people's example. In the whole of the developmental process from baby to 'elder', it is in *this* phase, between about eighteen months and three years, coinciding as it does with a rapidly-growing self-awareness, that 'aggressive behaviour' emerges and then reaches its peak. As long as the child receives the right kind of guidance, this aggression will gradually subside.

To adult eyes the behaviour which is so characteristic of this 'pre-school puberty' can sometimes be seen as manipulative. The fact is that small children cannot yet reflect upon their behaviour and cannot yet put themselves in another person's place. They are egocentric, not in a calculated way, but because they are not yet cognitively and emotionally mature enough to experience or show empathy. They have not yet developed a Superego or an Ego and, although they are starting to move in that direction, they cannot yet control their impulses: they are dependent upon caregivers and others in their world to help them to do this. In this phase the environment is particularly important in determining self-image and the (later) ability to deal with impulses, particularly aggressive ones. Children adopt the language and actions of the significant adults around them as their own: the function of these adults as behavioural models is crucial. Children see themselves first and foremost through the eyes of their caregivers, so if these adults frequently find fault with them they will see themselves as burdensome and unlovable.

> *A child who is frequently punished and treated as unlovable does not learn to overcome aggressive feelings, but instead experiences a build-up of aggression which he may later turn against himself or others.*

Children who feel loved, and are given the boundaries they need by adults who respect their children's integrity and *their* boundaries, will develop a sense of self-worth and will instinctively learn to channel their aggressive impulses.

If children feel good about themselves and are supported by positive role models, they will with the help of their own developing Super Ego, learn to harness their aggression, to control it and to transform it into constructive energy and action.

3.2.1 Self-image mirrored

Within every adult there is a child: this might be a child who was allowed to exist, a child who was over-idealized, a child who was only allowed to exist conditionally or a child who was never seen at all. This child influences our self-image as adults, the way in which we manage aggression, our beliefs and convictions, our projections and our actions. Adults who are 'seen' as children generally have a better chance of managing both their own aggression and that of others; they will be better at making an accurate assessment of other people's intentions and at deferring or even relinquishing the immediate gratification of their needs: in other words, they will have built for themselves a sound base from which they will be able to tolerate frustration.

Children who are excluded, abused or ill-treated will in the first few years of their lives see this as the natural way of things. All children, consciously or unconsciously, expect love and care from their parents. If they are not seen, taken seriously nor respected, this will become for them what love means. Children who are not seen can, in the course of their development and later as adults, suffer serious disturbances in their experience of themselves and of the world. Such adults may develop what we might call a defective 'love-programme': 'Love is being hit.' 'If my partner doesn't hit me, it means he doesn't love me.' 'Parents who don't hit their kids are a soft touch, they just get walked over.' 'Children who get hit are asking for it.' 'Parents who give their growing children a loving kiss goodbye and wave them off at the front door – well it's not healthy is it?'

When children who have been emotionally and physically neglected realize that their upbringing is or was far from natural, the first thing they do is blame themselves. 'If I hadn't been such a little monster, they would have loved me.' To state this unequivocally: the love-programme of a cherished child or a cherished adult is very different from that of a damaged child, and each love-programme will be associated with very different expectations of and projections upon the surrounding world.

3.2 The child position within Transactional Analysis

Transactional Analysis, a psychological system developed by Eric Berne in the 1950's, shares with psychoanalysis the concept of a threefold personality. Berne calls the three parts 'states of being': the *Parent* (comparable with the Superego), the *Child* (comparable with the Id) and the *Adult* (comparable with the Ego). Berne suggests that as individuals we present ourselves to others from a particular position or state of being: that of the Parent, the Adult or the Child. So in our interactions we respond to each other from the perspective of one of these three states and these responses are called '*transactions*'. Transactional Analysis offers us a clear and relatively tangible model for looking at (professional) relationships and at the concepts of transference and countertransference.

The parent

In the Parent (P) state of being we are:
- like our parents or caregivers as we experienced them
- as our parents would have liked us to be – what was the ego-ideal, the values and the 'shoulds', which were imparted to us during our upbringing?
- the authority figure, parent or caregiver we now wish to be

The Parent state of being consists of two components: the caring or nurturing parent (NP) and the controlling or critical parent (CP).

Transference and countertransference

The child

In the Child (C) state of being, the person is the little boy or the little girl we once were. The Child consists of three elements:
- obedient, compliant, watchful, *adaptive* (Adaptive Child: AK);
- recalcitrant, angry, resistant, *rebellious* (Rebellious Child: RK);
- spontaneous, playful, confident, natural, *free* (Free Child: FC).

The adult

In the Adult state of being, we are able to:
- make objective choices
- assimilate information
- mediate between our *own* Parent and Child, in other words the Parent within us and the Child within us

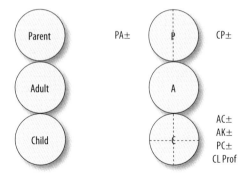

The little professor

The little professor is, as it were, the adult in the child. As children we create the little professor in order to protect ourselves. The little professor's job is to find answers to questions. Small children, who are not yet able to formulate all the questions they have, use their little professor to try and find explanations for things they do not yet understand. Small children who are secure will ask lots of questions and will receive answers to most of their questions and yet they will still not be able to understand the world around them completely.

Small children who are not secure will not receive answers to their questions and will learn to stop asking them; they will then be compelled to protect themselves and may have to spend more time dreaming and fantasizing in order to create a viable world for themselves.

Small children with predominantly happy parents will feel secure and will not have to expend energy looking for the reasons for their happiness; they will feel free to explore the world, to acquire knowledge and to develop a sense of independence.

Small children with predominantly unhappy, angry or rejecting parents will feel the need to try and find the cause of their behaviour. They will link this behaviour with their own person because their caregivers display it when they are around. They do not know that it has more to do with their caregivers' own emotions at that moment, with their childhood, or in extreme cases with traumatic experiences from the past, than with them. The little professor will make sure that they spend energy in looking for possible ways of adjusting their own behaviour, in the usually vain hope of preventing the sad or angry behaviour of their caregivers. They may also make the decision to conform with the mirror image held up by their caregivers: 'Okay, I'm nothing but a nuisance, I tell lies, I don't know how to share and there are always rows when I'm around; that must be how I am then. No point in trying to behave any other way…'.

From a very young age children are capable of picking up their caregivers' signals and if necessary using these as the basis for a particular strategy, in some cases even a survival strategy. Alice Miller (*The Drama of the Gifted Child,* 1981) calls this ability 'giftedness': every child has an innate talent for empathy and for survival. She calls it a 'drama' – in other words life is seen as an unfolding tragedy in which we play the main part. If children (must) suppress too many feelings of sadness, disappointment and pain because their caregivers are not responsive to their feelings, *and* if at the same time they are unable to make their caregivers 'happy', then they will live with feelings of constant guilt. They run the risk of developing a negative self-image and if there is no one else in their environment who shows them understanding, this self-image will be constantly reinforced. In the adult this store of unconscious feelings will emerge in the form of projections, transference and countertransference.

The little professor makes sure that the child can keep control over impossible situations by, for example, taking very good care of the adult be they capable or not in the child's environment. The little professor helps the child to survive. 'If I make sure the house is tidy before Dad gets home from work, then maybe he won't be so angry with us.' 'If Mum's has too much to do she always starts sighing and then Dad shuts himself up in his room; that's not very nice for her, so I try to help her a lot.' 'If I ask Mum to read one more book to me, then at least I won't hear her crying downstairs in the living room.' 'If I tell jokes at the table then my parents won't notice my little brother so much and they won't get so cross with him.' 'When I grow up I'm going to be just like my (kind, lovely) Auntie Margot.'

> Not long ago a colleague came to see me and said that he'd come across a good example of the little professor. He had seen a cartoon in which a grandfather was walking along the street with his grandson of about six whose belief in Santa Claus was beginning to wear thin. Pointing to two Santa Clauses outside two different shops, the grandfather said to his grandson, 'You see, he *does* exist, there are even two of him!' My colleague saw this comical example of magical thinking on the part of the grandfather as an expression of the little professor. I didn't entirely agree with him, because the little professor is the adult in the child, not the child in the adult. I also couldn't detect any example of transference from the little professor, the child in the grandparent. Thinking about this amusing story, I did come up with a different example of the little professor within it. The grandson hears his grandfather and senses the hidden meaning in what he says: 'It would please me very much if you could believe in Santa Claus just a bit longer, you're growing up so quickly.' The little professor in the grandson could think: 'I'm very fond of my grandpa, so I'll do him the favour of letting him think that I still believe in Santa Claus.'

Transactions

Transactions is the name Berne gives to the social interactions which take place between people; we all respond to each other in word and deed from the position, or state of being, of the Parent, the Adult or the Child. Every action from the one evokes a reaction, verbal or non-verbal, from the other: this is a transaction.

> One colleague asks another: 'Am I going to get the minutes from yesterday's meeting too?' She asks it in a neutral tone, adult to adult, and will receive the minutes, very probably without any fuss.
> But what happens if the colleague asks it accusingly, with an undertone of: 'See? They forgot me *again* when the minutes were handed out!' This tone, coming from either the Critical Parent or (if said in a slightly more injured tone) the Rebellious Child, evokes a reaction which depends very much upon the susceptibilities of the 'accused' colleague. If he has a lot of Free Child within him, he is likely to name the feeling implied in the tone: 'Are you cross with me?' or he will make a joke in which the feedback is clear, for example, by jumping to attention and crying 'Yes, MA'AM!' If he has a lot of Adapted Child in him, he will probably feel guilty and rush off in search of the minutes. If the 'accusing' colleague evokes the Rebellious Child in the other, he will probably feel blamed and may react by saying that he will have to go and look for them and then 'forgetting' to do so. From the position of the Critical Parent the colleague might say 'I'm not sure I like your tone.' From the Nurturing Parent he might say: 'I did give them to you, you know. Shall I help you look for them?'

Every reaction, originating in one of the different states of being, will result in yet another kind of transaction, evoking as it does a different state of being in the other person.

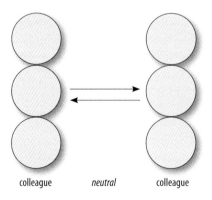

colleague   *neutral*   colleague

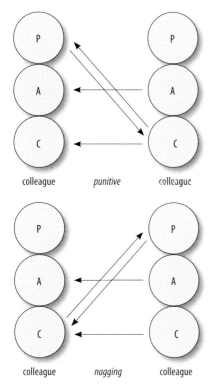

Transactional Analysis uses the terms *simple transactions* and *crossed transactions*. A simple reaction is a reaction which fits the expectation and matches the behaviour which evoked it. A Critical Parent calls upon the Adapted or the Rebellious Child. The other reacts from one of these two places: a simple transaction has occurred.

A crossed transaction is one which cuts across the expected reaction. If someone calls for adjustment, for instance, but instead of this the other responds from the position of the Adult or the Critical Parent, thereby cutting across the expected transaction, we get a crossed transaction.

> A father says to his child that he must clear his toys up (Critical Parent). The child obeys (Adjusted Child), the child does not hear because he's wholly involved in his play (Free Child) or he says that he doesn't feel like it (Rebellious Child). The child reacts from the Child to the Parent, a simple transaction.

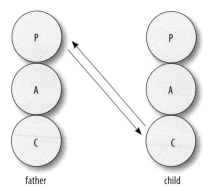

father   child

Imagine that the child reacts to his father by saying: 'You never clear up either, your socks and the newspaper and stuff, that's what Mum always says.' Then a crossed transaction would occur: the child reacts from the position of a critical and corrective parent to the Child in his father. In doing this he cuts across the transaction of his father, who of course expects a child's reaction.

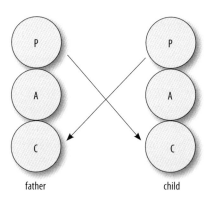

father   child

The father will now have to think about his answer- the following transaction. Does he react in a gruff and unfriendly way: 'And who do you think you're talking to, young man?' By doing this he 'punishes' the bit of Parent in the child: a reaction from the Critical Adult to the Child (in the child), a response which does not encourage the child to join in family life in an adult way. If he reacts from the position of the Nurturing Parent: 'Mm, well of course that must be a bit confusing for you. I'll give it some attention in future. But I am your dad, after all, aren't I? So how about clearing up quickly now,' then he remains in his role as father.

Or, if the father takes the opportunity to make an equal transaction of it, then he reacts from his own Adult to the Adult in the child and says: 'Well you know, you're quite right. Shall we do a deal: I clear up my stuff and you clear up your toys?'

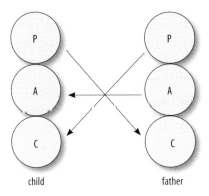

3.2.1 The TA perspective on transference

Transference is a transaction which originates in the Child within one person, who at a particular moment happens to feel dependent upon the other person within the relationship. In the example below transference explains why the expected transaction from the other is not answered but is cut across, resulting in a crossed transaction.

> Kitty receives a subscription to *Psychology* magazine from her friend Lisa. Lisa has been looking forward to giving this present and she had hoped that Kitty would be pleased. When Kitty opens the envelope she says: 'Oh, I've already got a subscription to *Psychology*, I've had one for years.' Lisa is disappointed and says that she didn't know this. Kitty reacts to this sharply and says: 'No, you wouldn't would you? Of course I've never been to university, so I certainly couldn't be expected to read a magazine like that…'. Lisa is completely taken aback by her friend's reaction.
> This is a crossed transaction: Lisa had expected pleasure and received a reprimand: the other's reaction cut across the expected emotional response. At the same time it is an example of transference: the first transactions are Adult to Adult, until Kitty directs her Rebellious Child reaction to-

wards her friend's Critical Parent – 'I expect you think I'm stupid, don't you?' Kitty reacts here out of an old feeling. She had an authoritarian father who, far from giving her the feeling that she was valued, treated her without respect and humiliated her. Although Kitty's mother was an intelligent woman, the only model she provided for her daughter was one of wordless submission to her husband's wishes. Her parents did not give Kitty the opportunity to study and as a result she feels at a disadvantage; this is a source of great pain to her. What Kitty does here is to project old anger which is actually intended for her parents, together with her own, personal sense of inferiority about being less educated than other people, from her Child onto Lisa. Kitty attributes to Lisa the feeling that her father once gave her and concludes that Lisa probably thinks she is stupid. She then adds to this the idea which she has developed over the years that people think you're stupid if you haven't been to university *and* ontop of this, her own anger about the whole situation.

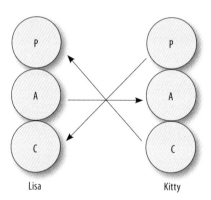

According to TA, transference within relationships originates in the person's (unfree) Child. The Child reacts to the Parent of the other person. Whilst Lisa thought she was interacting with Kitty from an Adult state of being, Kitty reacted to the Parent in Lisa: within any adult transaction the Child can suddenly put in an appearance, in word, tone or deed, and take the other by surprise. This child-response will always be coloured, at least to a certain extent, by parental influences from the past. Kitty's double message comes from both the Child and the Critical Parent in her. She is saying two things to her friend at the same time: 'How stupid of you to buy this kind of present for me!' and 'Can't you understand how hurtful it is to buy this kind of present for me?'

Maria and Julia have been good friends for years; they are both social workers. Maria has been married for many years and Julia lives alone. From time to time they go away somewhere together for a few days' break.

Julia had a cold, aloof mother who Julia feels was never there when she needed her. She has in the meantime broken all contact with her mother. Whilst Julia comes across as a robust and sociable person, there has always been an insecure, abandoned little girl hiding away inside her. Sometimes she seems insatiable for attention and she really does need a lot of it from her friend.

At a certain period in their friendship Julia is suffering from a lengthy bout of depression whilst Maria is having a particularly busy time with her husband, her job and her five-year-old son. When she can't quite manage to cope on her own, Julia goes to stay with Maria for a few days and then returns to her own home when she feels she can. On one of these occasions four days have passed and Maria has not been in touch with Julia. Maria is extremely busy and cannot manage for the moment to take care of her friend ontop of everything else. When Maria rings her at the end of the fourth day, a furious Julia picks up the phone: 'You weren't there when I needed you! Nobody's ever been there for me! I knew it, I said to myself - they'll just leave me in the lurch as usual! I always have to come to you, you never come to me, never ever…'. Maria is taken aback by her friend's reaction, but it also makes her angry. She tries to stay calm but at the same time to make it clear to Julia that she does not feel in any way that she has neglected her, but that just at this particular time she has a great deal in her own life which requires her attention.

The Child in Julia blames the Parent in Maria for not being willing to look after her, 'whilst she needs her so much.' This is a reproach from the Child in Julia intended for her mother and it is not congruent with Maria's behaviour; Maria had shown herself more than willing to offer adult care to her adult friend. Julia projects onto Maria an old feeling of abandonment which in fact belongs to her and particularly to the Child in her; this feeling is a very deeply-rooted one, but it does not match her present situation. Her feelings of abandonment cannot be met by the other people in her present life. Julia will have, as it were, to learn to take care of herself from her own Nurturing Parent; she will have learn to be a mother to herself.

This situation leads to a permanent rift in the friendship. As far as Julia is concerned it's all over; she will never be able to rely on Maria again.

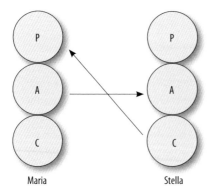

Maria   Stella

3.2.2   The TA perspective on countertransference

Countertransference is a transaction which originates in the Child of an 'authority figure'. The 'authority figure' feels a sudden dependency upon the more dependent other within the relationship. In such a case we react to an transaction from a client or an employee out of our own Child or Parent position and in doing so we cut across the other's expectations, or otherwise respond in an unprofessional way to the other's transaction.

> A client is late for an appointment, most unusually for her; this client happens to be a perfectionist and as a rule would much prefer to arrive too early than too late. The care worker has for some time found himself irritated by this client: she is a bit of a control-freak, just like his mother. Sometimes she even gives him headache: a case of countertransference.
> 'Sorry I'm late', says the client, Adult to Adult. In a very irritable and humourless tone the care worker says from his Critical Parent: 'The fact that we are working on your need for control doesn't mean that you have to be late!'
> The client is startled by this brusque reaction. She feels attacked and no longer able to speak as freely as she has done in other sessions. Apparently she has done something wrong but she is not sure exactly what, because the care worker has not made it clear to her in so many words. She's already so afraid of getting things wrong in other people's eyes -her transference. After all, she's not a perfectionist (or a control freak as the worker sees her) for no reason! She always does her very best to be one step ahead of any criticism! Now she stops taking any initiative, out of the Adapted Child position. And this just when she was beginning to feel a little less inhibited!

Here then, the care worker's countertransference has a negative effect upon the client's feeling of security and therefore upon her progress.

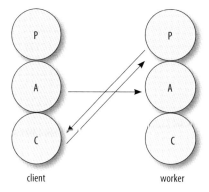

client   worker

> Rascha is a student of about twenty-five. She works at a children's day care centre and attends college one day a week. She is following a psychology class; the subject of this class is the toddler phase. The lecturer suggests that this stage can be a difficult one for students who work with this age-group, because these toddlers are busy developing their self-will. Suddenly they appear to be able to say 'no' and what is more they discover that this has an impact on the world around them: it makes something happen, a fantastic new experience! This phase is sometimes known as the 'terrible twos'; it is a challenging time for parents and practitioners alike: What is the best way to deal with it?
> Rascha says that at her day care she has no problem with this at all and she cites an example. David, a little boy of two-and-a-half, had declared that he didn't want to go outside today: Free Child or Rebellious Child. She had reacted angrily to this, saying: 'It is not up to you!' and had just picked the struggling, protesting child up and marched outside with him. 'Simple as that', she added crisply.
> Rascha comes from a family in which 'It was not up to her'. When she was five she was made to go and live with an aunt for a time without having any say in the matter. When she asked questions about it she was told that she should show more respect, that it was for her own good and who was she to think she knew better? 'Sometimes you just don't have any say in the matter' has become Rascha's point of view. She is extremely irritated

by children who have a will of their own. Acting out of her own Child, who is angry with the people who brought her up, she reacts to David in a rather unprofessional way.

In the same week, Rascha was picked up from the day care by a cousin. A little boy of almost four asked her: 'Is that your boyfriend?' She reacted angrily to the child: 'You don't ask a person who is older than you are questions like that!'

Rascha projects her own childhood self-image 'I have no say in the matter' and 'I have no respect if I ask questions' onto children. The message she conveys to them, from her bit of Critical Parent, is: 'You have no say in the matter and if you ask questions or don't see things as I do, then you have no respect for me'. Unconsciously she transfers her helplessness as a child and her rage about this (stored in her Child), as well as her imprinted image about how 'parents' behave (stored in her Critical Parent) onto David and other children, who in their turn have no say in the matter: countertransference.

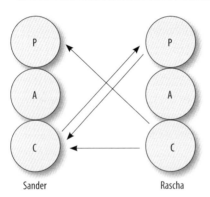

Sander   Rascha

3.2.3 The little professor

As a small child we all carry in us an adult part who attempts to understand and to make sense of the adult world in which we find ourselves. The Adult in the Child, whom we are calling the little professor, asks questions and tries to give things some kind of order and predictability. The little professor in the child can offer protection in an insecure environment; he will do this by trying to understand his caregivers to such an extent that he is able to anticipate, prevent or limit unsafe situations.

The role played by the little professor in our youth is by no means over by the time we reach adulthood. Remnants of the little professor can be detected in projections and transference processes.

Transference will already occur in children who are (temporarily) dependent upon the care of people other than their original caregivers. In the first place this happens simply as a result of their basic needs as children but it will also arise from the expectations which they have already developed towards adults. Undamaged children will react to adults from a basis of trust. They expect adults to respond to them with respect and they will react with surprise if this proves not to be the case. In the example above, David would be more likely to be surprised than hurt by Rascha's behaviour – that is, if it is markedly different from that of his parents – because the behaviour would not answer his expectations. If David himself comes from an authoritarian, unresponsive family, then Rascha's behaviour would be familiar to him: it would match his expectations. He would be more likely to be confused if he were *not* reprimanded, because he would then feel that he was not being offered clear boundaries. We are talking here about *unconscious* processes: children are able to survive, but they cannot yet *consciously* manipulate their environment.

> Ellis is the daughter of fairly well-off parents. She is seven years old and is in year three at a primary school in a small town. Up until now her father's work has taken Ellis and her family to various parts of the world for differing lengths of time. For a while now they have been living in the the Netherlands. Ellis has moved several times in the course of her short life; she has frequently had to part from children who had become her friends. She now holds back a little from making contact in what is for her yet another year-group. She has become used to spending a great deal of her time on her own.
> Ellis' family situation is secure. Because it was for her the one stable place in the midst of all the moving, her family is her 'safe niche'. Ellis' basic feeling has from the start been one of respect and security, so when she finds herself being left out at her new school, her first response is one of astonishment. She cannot understand why the other children do not accept her or help her to find her place in their year-group. When she is mocked

because she speaks 'posh', the members of staff do not intervene. The other pupils say things like: 'Your mother's stuck-up,' and the underlying message seems to be: 'I don't understand how you can want her for a mother….'. Ellis cannot comprehend why the children would say this sort of thing. It sounds very spiteful and, anyway, she loves her mother. Ellis is confused: the behaviour of the children and the teachers does not match her expectations.

One day Thomas, one of Ellis' classmates is handing out books in the classroom and Ellis is missed out. She puts her hand up to tell the teacher. The teacher says: 'Oh Thomas, are you going to give Her Royal Highness a book too?' Ellis drops a curtsey, thanks him for the book and after school runs home in tears. From that moment on, Ellis decides to find all her security at home. Her home-life becomes a safe haven against the threat of the school-situation. Her little professor says: 'There's something very wrong here. These teachers and those children are unkind, don't expect anything more from them.'

Years later Ellis is in her early twenties; the course she is following requires her to make a choice out of several main subjects: massage, homeopathy, alternative medicine and person-centred counselling. She receives supervision to help her with her study, her practical training and the setting up of her own practice. Her supervisor asks her why she has not chosen counselling as her main subject: it seemed to her just the thing for Ellis. 'Yes, one of my other teachers said the same thing', replied Ellis, 'but it's not for me, all that rooting about in your childhood.' The supervisor, surprised at the fierceness of her reaction, starts to probe a bit further- carefully, so as not to root about… and in the course of the conversation it emerges that Ellis is extremely reluctant to speak about her home-situation. She is terrified that other people will try, just as the children in her class with their 'your mother's stuck-up' once did, to convince her that her childhood and her parents were not nearly as nice as she thought they were. She cherishes and defends her childhood and her home-life as if it were a hoard of priceless treasure. Ellis transfers an old feeling onto her supervisor: the feeling, the fear, that the supervisor will try to rob her of her safe haven, just as the children and staff at school once did. Searching questions about her childhood put her immediately on the defensive and very nearly on the attack. This sensitive area has a direct effect on Ellis' freedom

> of choice within her studies. Her little professor is still fulfilling a function which is in fact redundant because her supervisor and others have no wish to rob her of her positive image of home. Her little professor still offers her protection in situations where it is no longer necessary.

Many children who do not get what they need at home can sometimes make use of a healthy survival mechanism, *compensation*, to 'take on board' warmth and security from, say, their friends' parents or their teachers. They make healthy use of what is a survival strategy – their little professor. Children who can compensate are in a position to be able to construct a concept of trust for themselves: from a basis of mistrust the potential for trust, although vulnerable, will be available to them because the Adult in the Child has registered the fact that things can be different.

> Since the age of three Melanie has been the victim of physical, sexual and emotional abuse. She often stays with various aunts and uncles whilst her mother is in hospital recovering from the effects of her father's violence. Her father drinks, her mother is unable to protect Melanie from his rages, and one of the uncles with whom she stays regularly has been abusing her since she was three – and her mother *must* have known about this. Home is an unsafe place for all the children and Melanie is not safe with her relatives either. When Melanie is at primary school and later at secondary school, she often spends time at a friend's house. The atmosphere there is warm and happy; to her surprise the friend's father does not come home drunk every day; her mother asks her own children and Melanie how school was, and what is more listens to what they have to say. Melanie realizes that things can be different from the way they are at home and this realization is enough to keep her going. An early adult bit of her, her little professor, provides her with some hope for the future. As an adult, studying, working and undergoing therapy, she is extremely cautious about placing her trust in others and within her friendships she always remains vulnerable, but she has managed to learn the ability to trust.
>
> In therapy, the female therapist listens carefully to her story – the early abuse, the emotional and physical damage, the repeated humiliations.

The therapist is struck by the way in which Melanie tends to play down her painful memories – it could all have been so much worse. And anyway she was a troublemaker, that's what they always said… Here too her little professor has played his part, but this time in a counter-productive way: she was a troublemaker and that's why they hit her. There was no other way in which Melanie as a child could make sense of the behaviour of her extremely damaged parents. At least this way there was a certain logic to it.

Even in the safety of the therapy room she always sits facing the door: you have to be on the watch for who might come in. She shrinks from telling her therapist the details of the abuse she suffered. Melanie has been protecting her mother for years; she thought that if she had told her what was going on, her mother would not have been able to cope – she was so often ill as it was. She transfers this feeling onto her therapist: it's too much, I shall spare you the details, you wouldn't be able to cope with them. At the same time Melanie is afraid, deep in her heart, that the therapist will say: 'You're sniveling, are you? I'll give you something to snivel about!' and throw her out of the room or humiliate her in front of the other children: that's what her father did if she was frightened or sad. Melanie expects her therapist to think that she 'has no reason to start sniveling', in the same way that her parents and relatives always ridiculed her grief.

These transference feelings impede her progress. Gaining insight into these transference issues will be for her the stepping stones to change and will lead to her being able to recover her integrity. Taking her own feelings of grief, terror and humiliation seriously and allowing herself to really feel them will give her the impetus to integrate them and become whole. Melanie will have to accept that she, as someone who has been seriously abused, is suffering from post-traumatic stress, whereby she is and *must be* permanently alert and on her guard. She will have to recognize just how painful and humiliating her childhood really was. She will have to try to let go of the survival mechanism which protected her when she was totally dependent but which now no longer serves its purpose. She no longer needs to be constantly vigilant, to keep all the doors open or to watch them constantly; she must, as it were, dare to open and close doors. Only then can she start to work through her grief; she needs to make the pain available to her Child by letting go of her survival mechanism.

The capacity for loyalty which children have towards their parents is limitless; it is exactly this which makes things so confusing for the child. To say 'My father was unable to love me, but it wasn't anything I did' or 'My mother was just wrapped up with herself all the time, nothing we did was ever good enough, but it wasn't my fault' is too much to ask of the loyal child. And yet this was the reality. In order to work things through you have to look in a different way at the people who brought you up. These people, who were responsible for you, made mistakes which resulted in their damaging you. They probably did this out of powerlessness, but this does not take away from the fact that these people who brought you up were adults and they should have taken care of you, however difficult they may have found you. Only by thinking like this can you begin to see yourself differently, to clear yourself of blame, certainly as far as your childhood years are concerned. But this takes time…

Damaged children will in the first instance respond to other adults or substitute caregivers out of feelings of mistrust or resignation: 'You won't take me seriously; you're not to be trusted; if I place my trust in you, you'll shame me'. Such children were neither seen nor understood by those who were responsible for their upbringing. It is as if at a very young age damaged children develop an adult part from which they attempt to comprehend their parents' thinking in the effort to be one step ahead of their often unpredictable or malicious behaviour. This premature development of an adult within the child, a 'too grown-up' little professor, means that s/he cannot be the naturally free yet dependent child s/he really is and will therefore miss out one or more of the developmental stages: s/he will have lost the ability be a spontaneous child at play. When children like this are at last able to find security somewhere, it is very likely that they may regress to a stage which in terms of age they have already passed; this is because they have only now found the safety which they so badly needed at this earlier stage. Later on these children or adults may display excessively dependent or demanding behaviour in relation to their supervisors or social care workers. The powerful transference and countertransference of such feelings of dependency, in parent-child, adult-child as well as in adult-adult contact, can lead to problems in professional relationships.

3.3 Conscious and unconscious projection

Young people and adults alike transfer feelings from their child – the child within them who has felt and still feels misunderstood, ignored or abandoned- onto others.
Boswijk-Hummel (1997) states in her book *Liefde in Wonderland (my translation)*:
'It is the child in the client who does the projecting. The greater the pain, the greater will be the need for support and the more powerful the tendency to project. Feelings of loneliness often stem from very earliest babyhood. The continuing presence of the child reveals itself principally in the occasional (or regular) emergence of these early feelings in the here-and-now. People who have felt abandoned as a baby, for instance, will as adults very easily feel let down by others. Being alone evokes feelings of fear in them and they have difficulty being on their own; they will always tend to seek company. The early emotions appear in the present when the present situation is similar to the early situation. It is on the basis of these emotions that projection occurs.'

We all carry with us memories and emotions which colour new situations. Some memories are relatively easy to make conscious.

Hanna's father used to smoke a pipe. The smell of pipe-tobacco always gives Hanna a good feeling. It reminds her of her carefree childhood. In later life this positive association will colour her initial response to every pipe-smoking man she meets. The memory of a living room with a wood-burning stove, a kind, reassuring father and the play of sunlight through the conservatory window will be transferred randomly onto every man who happens to smoke a pipe. Hanna's (old) feeling has nothing to do with the man in the present situation: it is her projection. She is aware of this association, it is a conscious one. She knows that pipe-smoking in itself does not confer upon the man the qualities she attributes to her father; and yet she still, however fleetingly, experiences this feeling.

Naima's father also smokes a pipe. When her father, a dark-haired, burly man, was at home, a deathly hush would fall on the house. The tension

> was palpable – the children all walked around on tiptoe. One false move or comment could trigger an outburst of rage from her father: this was *his* house, *he* hadn't asked for these children and why had God punished him with such brats…?' The children would take refuge in their rooms, but even there they were not always safe. Naima is very wary of dark, thick-set men. She expects unpredictable behaviour from such men and does not dare to trust them. The smell of pipe smoke makes her extremely agitated. Naima knows that these feelings are not realistic, that they are only old feelings, but she still experiences them.

Some memories are more difficult to bring into consciousness. An example:

> A male student of twenty-eight says that he finds my male colleague John creepy. This surprises me. John is a respectful, kind, fatherly, somewhat older man with a beard – in my eyes the very image of a trustworthy lecturer. Whilst talking with this student it emerged that John in his role as lecturer and mentor had in the course of a conversation about his progress put a hand on the student's shoulder, undoubtedly with the intention of reassuring him – things were for various reasons not going too well at the time. During a psychology lesson he had been confronted with issues from his past which had disturbed and confused him and, noticing this, John had made time to speak to him at the end of the college day. The student had felt relatively secure with John as mentor of his year group – until this last conversation. He already found the fact that John had made so much room for him a reason for suspicion. When John put a hand on his shoulder he knew it for sure: 'Don't trust this man!' He now even starts to think that it was stupid of him ever to have trusted John in the first place: he'd fallen for it again. It appears that as a young boy in the children's home where he lived, this student was subjected to abuse by one of the group leaders- an older man with a beard: 'The same sort of creep as John with that smarmy, sympathetic tone of his'. The student was not conscious of this association with the past.
> The student remains wary of John, even after consciously identifying the

> source of his feeling. It is difficult for him to let go of the feelings which John evokes in him. There is evidence here of a major disturbance in the projection: the student transfers old, unassimilated feelings onto a teacher who is in reality trustworthy and upon whom he feels dependent: transference.

Boswijk-Hummel considers the longing for security, warmth and unconditional acceptance which shows itself in relationships to be a primal longing which will manifest itself in every partner-relationship. It will in fact emerge in any relationship in which dependency plays a part. The intensity of the hunger for recognition from the other or others, as well as the nature of any disturbance in a person's projections, will however be determined by his or her childhood experiences.

Adult dependency carries the memories within it of earlier relationships with parents, caregivers and teachers. In all work situations in which any kind of hierarchy exists, there will also be a degree of mutual dependency: this provides fertile ground for the transfer of old conscious and unconscious feelings. If trust has been internalized, that is, if feelings of trust have been so far integrated as to provide a solid basis, then this trust will form the ground for projections within further relationships. If mistrust has been internalized- if feelings of mistrust have been integrated as to the basis, then mistrust will provide an obviously less fertile and less secure ground. For those who work in counselling and care professions, the importance of making transference issues as conscious as possible cannot be overemphasized.

3.4 Transference and family role

In *Liefde in Wonderland*, Boswijk-Hummel discusses the way in which children try to win the attention of their parents in the family context. To do this children often develop ways of behaving which will distinguish them from their siblings. This personal, functional behaviour can be reinforced until it becomes a powerful specialization. The uncomplicated child with the sunny disposition does not need to do much more than to carry on behaving as s/he has always done. Children who are quick learners only need to bring their report home to get the applause. The funny, charming child knows how to steal the show from day one. But it can sometimes be the case that after a while a child needs to develop new behaviour, because getting attention with the behaviour which came easily no longer works. Some children try to be noticed by behaving in a thoughtful and diligent way, others will try not to be noticed by making themselves invisible, and yet others try to get attention from parents and the environment as a whole by displaying 'problem' behaviour. In this way we develop a system whereby our own behaviour, which we are by nature good at, is supplemented with survival behaviour which is intended *either* to gain the attention of our caregivers *or* to protect ourselves against them. This transference of the family role can become visible in the way clients behave towards one another and towards authority figures in a group-setting. In a similar way family roles can become visible within a team of professional practitioners, both in their behaviour towards one another and in relation to their supervisors.

Boswijk-Hummel divides the different ways of trying to get attention and esteem into four broad categories:

1. Being nice: asking for attention by adapting, doing your best, being helpful and supportive.
2. Being good at something: winning attention by excelling yourself, achieving, getting good marks.
3. Making trouble: demanding attention by causing problems.
4. Not attracting attention: being as invisible as possible.

> Mary is twenty-six. She participates in group-supervision as part of her training as a social care practitioner. From the start Mary is wary of her female supervisor. She is worried that she will say something stupid and that her supervisor will reject her if she speaks honestly about herself, about her insecurities and about the things which concern her. At the same time Mary puts the supervisor on a pedestal and expects support and acknowledgement from her. This transference receives attention and is discussed and clarified, as a result of which the supervision group becomes a more secure place for Mary.
>
> Mary was born in Suriname. As the only one of her large family she was given away to a childless aunt in the Netherlands. This aunt, her foster mother, was strict and aloof: she offered her all the opportunities which

Mary would never have had in Suriname so Mary *had* to achieve. Who she *was* was not important, it was what she *did* that mattered. And yet nothing that Mary worked so hard to achieve in her young life was ever good enough. She did her best to adapt herself to what was expected of her and never rebelled, but still her foster mother never gave her the feeling that she was loved.

As an adult Mary has a difficult relationship with her foster mother and her contact with her birth-mother seems to be damaged beyond repair; Mary feels that she has been discarded.

In the meantime she has two children of her own, a boy and a little girl, Anna, aged five. During the supervision Mary says that she feels guilty because she does not love the little girl as much as the boy, and this whilst Anna does so much for her. As young as she is, Anna knows just what her mother needs; she helps her around the house and is always by her side. It is unbearable for Mary to see herself in her own early family role: Anna makes every attempt to win her mother's love, just as Mary herself tried to do with her foster mother and also later with her biological mother. To see and experience this in relation to Anna is extremely painful for her. In fact Mary sometimes has the urge to push this emotionally very gifted little girl away… In the supervision they discuss the fact that Anna is very like the little Mary: well-adapted, sweet, obliging, and that Mary is now transferring the rejection she received from her foster mother onto Anna. Mary rejects the child in herself and can therefore not enjoy little Anna: countertransference. Were Mary to look clearly at Anna and to realize how hard Anna has to work to gain her love, she would be grief-stricken. Mary protects herself against this grief by closing herself off from her daughter and in so doing she is unable to feel any love for her. She can, however, feel love for her son, because he is less threatening.

Mary enters therapy. She learns to look at herself and to understand that it was not her fault that she was not loved, but that this was to do with her caregivers' limitations. She is now experiencing the same limitations in her love for her own daughter.

A little further into the therapy, Mary tries to talk to Anna about how 'Mummy has made some silly mistakes, but Mummy really does love her very much.' Anna says understandingly, 'Oh never mind Mummy, I do that sometimes too.' Mary also tries to set limits on some of the many things

> that the five-year-old does for her around the house: 'But Mummy', says Anna every time, 'I *like* doings things for you.' Anna has already internalized – integrated into herself – a pattern of taking care of her mother and being seen to be doing so, but in contrast with the earlier role which Mary played, Anna's role can now be acknowledged and talked about, and is therefore likely to be less tenacious and less damaging. Mary has room to breathe and so has Anna.

3.5 Positive and negative transference

Boswijk-Hummel (1997) draws a distinction between positive and negative transference. In her view positive transference is the projection of the ideal father or mother upon the social care practitioner: the client transfers onto the worker his childhood wishes about his caregiver as he would have liked him to be. This can bring with it feelings of dependency, the need to hold on, the need for security, the longing for nurturing and admiration, even the feeling of being in love.

Negative transference is the projection of the unsafe, inadequate, rejecting parent onto the social care worker. The client transfers his child's lingering negative feelings towards the person who brought him up. This negative transference can bring with it feelings of fear, insecurity, loneliness and anger.

Whilst some forms of transference and countertransference can be separately identified as positive or negative, it is more common for these two aspects to be closely interwoven.

Looking at Mary's story, it is clear that the transference in it is neither wholly positive nor wholly negative. Mary projects onto her supervisor the expectation that she will be rejected and already talks angrily about this with fellow students before the supervision even begins: a case of negative transference. At the same time Mary seeks approval and recognition from her supervisor and looks up to her because she also experiences her as someone to be trusted and relied upon: a case of positive transference.

The countertransference in relation to Anna is negative: Mary's old childhood feelings of powerlessness, rage and rejection are contained in it, but at the same time so is the positive expectation that the child will give her unstinting love; and because young children have the innate capacity to do this, then this is exactly what Anna does.

Perhaps it also useful to mention here how ordinary, everyday transference works. We are talking here about the whole reservoir of childhood experiences which facilitate us in our daily lives in countless ways, which provide us with information about the different social situations we find ourselves in, which help us to move effortlessly into the role of pupil when we want to learn something or to take on the role of a worker under the leadership of a supervisor. They enable us to form love-relationships, to become parents to our children and to fulfill an authority-role when this is required of us. We all have at our disposal a vast, unconscious store of childhood experiences which we can easily put to use in many different educational and work-related situations. In this book we turn our attention specifically to the kind of transference and countertransference which sooner hinders than facilitates our relationships with others and which interferes with our own or the other's progress and development. Becoming aware of this transference and countertransference, and learning to deal with its various manifestations in oneself and in the other person, can be a fascinating and rewarding process. It can give an extra dimension to our contact with others and can enrich the quality of our interactions.

In the following chapter we will elucidate the concepts of transference and countertransference by examining some of the aspects which are typically encountered in daily professional practice.

Defining features in daily practice 4

Transference and countertransference in practice

Counselling, care work, supervision, coaching, guidance and management have a common feature, which is the fact that there is a certain degree of inequality involved: it is a case of one person being guided and the other doing the guiding. The former is to a greater or lesser extent dependent upon the latter; the practitioner does have a certain kind of 'power' because it is s/he who provides the quality of guidance and in the early stages, determines the nature of the relationship. The client or worker is more likely to 'wait and see what happens', at least at first.

We can also speak of mutual dependency, between coach and client and between supervisor and worker, in the sense that the one role cannot exist without the other and both roles lend their own colour to the relationship. This mutual dependency displays features of earlier roles, for instance, between parent or caregiver and child. Parents take the lead and determine the way in which the child is brought up, but the child determines how s/he responds to their lead. In this sense the child, client or worker also has 'power'.

In the previous chapter we looked at family roles. Children will make a certain role their own in order to ensure the attention or protection of their caregivers. Such a role, which may not necessarily be a functional one, can then be developed as a way of manipulating their responses. Both functional and non-functional features of these past family roles will affect the dynamic between client and practitioner, between supervisor and worker, between worker and co-worker; these features will show themselves in the behaviour of both parties in positive and negative ways.

In the following section we shall be examining several aspects which could be said to characterize the dynamics within working relationships and these include: working with objectives, interaction, punctuation, content and context, closeness and distance and dependency. These will be illustrated with examples from daily practice in which transference and countertransference plays a part.

4.1 Working with objectives

Every form of counselling has its own objectives. The nature of these objectives will depend upon the needs and potential capacities of particular clients and of particular teams or organizations. Leadership roles are currently seen in terms of human resource management or coaching; this shift in definition indicates a shift in the nature of working relationships. The concepts 'adjustment' and 'rehabilitation' within a welfare context have developed under the influence of new social theory into *personal development* and *the nurturance of talents*. There has been a shift from a group-directed approach towards a more individually-oriented one: this is, for instance, reflected in individual budgeting for people with an intellectual disability, and certainly within all other areas of the care sector there is a trend towards customized care which strives to give clients the chance to opt for the care which is best suited to their needs. All these measures are directed towards maintaining the capacities and independence of clients to the maximum. By contrast, we can see in young offenders' institutions a movement towards a group-directed approach in order to stimulate the development of a sense of moral responsibility; within this sector too much personal freedom has been found to have a negative effect. It is clear that in every sector all kinds of changes are taking place, changes which are constantly making new demands upon practitioners who must adapt their personal capacities to the needs of the situation. This process requires continuous interaction: attunement with the client, consultation with staff and colleagues and the evaluation of objectives.

> Nancy works in psychiatric care. In her section a system of contracts is used to which both sides must adhere; the purpose of this system is to give clients as much responsibility as possible for their own recovery process. Nancy thinks that her colleagues are too hard on the clients in this; in fact she will (too) often arrange for clients things which in fact they could and should be doing for themselves. Because of this some of the clients tend to idolize her and always go to her for help or advice; Nancy is for them the mother they had always longed for: understanding, patient, warm – a clear case of transference.
> During staff meetings this situation is a regular subject for discussion: the fact that Nancy's attitude deviates from that of her colleagues means that the approach of the team as a whole towards the clients shows a lack of consistency. Some clients are confused by this and as a consequence try to manipulate some of the other members of staff; in fact not long ago a client had had an attack of rage with one of Nancy's colleagues and had had to be isolated; the attack had been triggered by a promise which Nancy had made to him but which was not allowed within the terms of his contract. Important objectives were not met in this case because Nancy had cut across the arranged agreement with her amenable and accommodating behaviour.
> Nancy thinks that her colleagues and also the psychiatrist don't understand the clients at all and they have no idea what they've been through and what they need; only she does. After a childhood in which nobody understood her, Nancy herself had a psychotic episode from which she recovered, so she knows exactly what the clients need! Above all they need warmth and understanding. Nancy's countertransference issue is that on the one hand her vulnerable Child is touched by her clients' vulnerability, and on the other hand she tries to 'score' off her clients: not only do they value her, they idolize her!

4.2 Continuous interaction

In care work, but also in many other professional situations, it is the continuous interaction between clients and practitioners which is the means by which objectives are met. This continuous interaction is central to care relationships and in this sense we are in a vulnerable area because the quality of care depends upon the professional attitude and standard of skill of the practitioner. An indifferent therapist who goes through the motions but cannot summon up any real interest in the client's unique story will not be able to offer the security which will enable the client to change. A teacher who only talks to pupils about their shortcomings, but forgets to mention what they do well, will not encourage learning. A group leader who isolates or punishes difficult youngsters for the slightest misdemeanor, but fails to provide a role model for them because he is just not kind enough, is not suited for work with young people with behavioural difficulties. Care-for-the-elderly practitioners who patronize their clients, and do everything for them because they think that the elderly should not have to make any effort, do not work to the objective of encouraging their clients to maintain their independence wherever possible. Managers, supervisors or coaches who have too little contact with their staff and who do not put in regular appearances on the work floor, will not be in a position to meet today's common objectives. Interaction is vital and must be qualitatively in order.

Interaction is the verbal and non-verbal communication with others. Continuously attuning oneself to other people is what makes care work attractive and at the same time arduous for practitioners; having an 'off' day will have a direct and immediate impact upon clients and co-workers. In one-to-one relationships it is perhaps possible to hide things, but working with groups leaves one much more vulnerable.
When you're having an off-day, usually well-behaved children start clinging and whining, your normally contented clients with an intellectual disability are unbelievably hard to please, your favourite colleague appears to walk past you without saying hello, the client who seemed to be making such progress says the therapy is a waste of time, your staff form a collective front against your new initiatives… and you… well, 'you are your own instrument'…

> Carol works in a residential group for older people with an intellectual disability, where continuous interaction and continuous intervention is the order of the day. Carol comes from Suriname originally and has very dark skin. During the supervision group she talks about a difference of opinion

> she has had with one of the older women; at the height of the argument the client had shouted: 'You stupid black woman, get back to your plantation!' 'Quite clever for a mentally disabled…' jokes one of the other students. Carol was worried that she had been too hard on this woman. She had always got on well with her, which is why she had felt cut to the quick by her remark; she simply hadn't seen it coming. Carol had in the past been cut to the quick often enough as one of the few children in her small town community who came from Suriname… At primary school and later on at the comprehensive she had had a few white friends, but when it came down to it she'd always had the feeling that she didn't really belong. She had reacted to this client out of the anger which arose from her old feeling of disillusionment.
>
> The sanction which Carol had imposed upon this woman was to withhold her usual ration of cigarettes; she was dependent upon Carol for her supply. This was how she had punished her; after a few hours the client had had to plead with her to lift the sanction. Afterwards Carol had regretted what she had done and now she wanted to know what the supervision group thought about it.
>
> Carol herself admitted that she had overreacted; the old pain of rejection because of her skin colour and the fact that she had got on so well with this client for years now and had not anticipated this rejection from her, had wounded her and made her act unreasonably: countertransference.

Continuous interaction makes a constant call upon any practitioner's skill, dedication and flexibility. In many management situations supervisors have to act as intermediaries between staff and management, whilst managers in their turn are expected to show tact and understanding in their search for compromises between at least two parties. This can all lead to stressful situations in which transference and countertransference can easily play their part. Middle-management functions can sometimes be compared with a mediating role between two conflicting parents: you can never get it right because according to each party your loyalty always lies with the other. Times of change can bring stress and the experience of constantly being under pressure and this can make practitioners vulnerable to an increased risk of the wrong sort of transference and countertransference.

Mike works in a general hospital as head of a department under which the social work section falls. Mike is fifty, whilst the rest of the social work team consists of women, of whom the youngest is fifty-seven. This team has a duty to offer rapid and effective care to patients before they are discharged and their efficiency in this has recently been the object of much criticism. The team members are unwilling to discuss this criticism and instead lay the blame for everything on staff shortages; they show themselves to be resistant to any self-appraisal. There is a lot of pressure on Mike from higher up to ensure that his team starts working more efficiently.

In a work-assessment meeting Mike decides to bring up the subject of 'maximizing efficiency' with the social work team. Within minutes the atmosphere has completely degenerated; the team accuses Mike of bad management – he should be demanding extra staff. Mike finds himself getting furious with them: he is not prepared to put up with this attitude for a moment longer! The team responds promptly by declaring a vote of no confidence in Mike; it all seems to be over within minutes.

Mike goes straight to Peter, his manager's office in an emotionally overwrought state; Peter, who knows him as an even-tempered, congenial team leader, is surprised to see him like this and he and Mike start to think about what might lie behind this uncharacteristic reaction. What emerges is that the attitude of his team evokes both helplessness and rage in Mike. The combined effect upon Mike of a number of disaffected women of a certain age is a powerful one: it reminds him of his mother. In the past, if Mike asserted an opinion of his own or disagreed with his mother, it would invariably end with a diatribe from her about 'why he found it so necessary to cause her pain'. She would then promptly retire to bed with a migraine. This left Mike with a dizzying mixture of guilt, anger and powerlessness.

The accusation by his team that he doesn't take care of them properly, combined with their refusal to reflect upon their own behaviour, triggers in Mike the same feelings of powerlessness. In recognizing this pitfall as countertransference, he is able to see an opening for further discussion with his team.

4.3 Punctuation

No one role can exist without the other and each role constantly influences the other: in the process of interaction mutual influence is continuously being exerted and shifts in one role have direct effect upon the other. When roles remain fixed for any length of time, a pattern emerges which creates a certain predictability in the interaction process. Patterns which repeatedly emerge are called *punctuation*. The word punctuation literally means 'markers in a text': full stops, commas, questions marks and exclamation marks are used to bring order to written language. When we speak of punctuation in communication and interaction what we mean is: how we bring order into the way we interact.

Supervisor and client, manager and team member are dependent upon each other for a particular product or outcome, be it growth, a behaviour-change, recovery, a pleasant stay, the acquisition of knowledge or emotional 'learning'. Co-workers are dependent upon each other for a productive working relationship. Within this continuous interaction, fixed patterns in communication can emerge, especially in a residential setting where people are in intensive daily contact with each other.

Sooner or later every relationship finds its own particular order: expectations evolve which give form to the interaction. If you have a question about a meeting that you've missed, you are unlikely to ask a colleague who you know will probably say: 'Oh, nothing ever happens in our meetings, does it?' or 'Oh! Weren't you there? I didn't notice.' You will ask a colleague from whom you expect to get an answer. Within groups the relationships find their own order fairly quickly, so in a team it is usually easy to detect a certain predictability. This offers security but sometimes also an order which can become fixed and fixing. Punctuation is the name given to a recurring pattern in communication.

> Not long ago Tina started working with a group of people with an intellectual disability. She likes the work but is not yet sure exactly what is expected of her. One group of residents are just back from work and Tina has made them a cup of tea and asked them how their day has gone. Just at that moment her supervisor comes in: 'Hello' she says, 'everything going okay?' Tina begins to blush: 'I'm just having a cup of tea,' she says, almost

> shamefacedly. 'So I see,' says the supervisor, smiling. She thinks: I'll bring this up later; she sees Tina was startled when she came in, but she has no idea why.
>
> Tina comes from a large family, where the children always had to be doing something. If you sat down on the sofa for a minute to think or to have a chat with a brother or sister, you would always hear: 'Haven't you got something better to do than sit around all day? Go and do something instead of hanging about being bored! Go and do the washing-up or some cleaning, or tidy your room …'. What her mother actually meant was: You're making me feel uncomfortable by sitting there because I have no idea what to do with you (no one has ever taught me). Of course Tina did not know this then. She felt uncomfortable if she ever took a moment to sit down and just stare into space, especially if anyone came in unexpectedly on one of these rare occasions and caught her doing nothing.
>
> So if she happens to be having a cup of tea, something which is in fact very nice for the residents, she thinks she's not 'working'. When she sees her supervisor, she expects her to be thinking: 'Go and get on with something, don't sit around being bored.'

We find the punctuation in Tina's reaction, who expects her supervisor to give her a telling off and reacts out of an old pattern: she becomes self-conscious when she sees her supervisor and gives the impression that she has been 'caught out': transference. This could evoke a complementary response in her supervisor: 'What's the matter here? Is everything okay?' If the punctuation in this relationship is not readjusted, a pattern could evolve whereby: the supervisor comes in, Tina is on the alert, the supervisor is on the alert, Tina is even more cautious, the supervisor becomes suspicious or reprimanding.

This supervisor, however, is an excellent coach who observes without making judgments. When she has a chance to speak to Tina she will share her observations with her: When I came in this afternoon I could see that you and the group were having a very nice time drinking tea together, but I thought you seemed a bit startled and nervous when I appeared. Is that right? I don't like the idea that I might make you feel nervous.'

Talking about behaviour which you notice and saying what the behaviour evokes in you with an 'I-message' can form an opening for talking about communication patterns; this in turn can offer the possibility of changing punctuation which limits and interferes with effective communication.

> A new manager is compelled to effect changes in the working methods of his team. The punctuation in the department is one of: 'Who does he think he is? The old one wasn't as bad as all that, even though we had a lot to complain about' set against the manager's take on the situation: 'This place has been in a mess for years, be grateful that I've arrived to make some changes around here.' The resistance sits like a sticky, stringy wad of gum in every meeting; every item on the agenda has to be chewed over endlessly, but nobody is ever satisfied – the chewing gum lost its flavour long ago.
> The only way to break through this punctuation is to name the resistance and to ask questions about it: How do we see each other? What do we expect of one another and how can we re-establish good working relationships? Being able to speak about underlying feelings- possible anger about years of bad management: 'We've never been taken care of properly before, so don't bother to start now,' and fear of change: 'Better to stay with parents who row all the time than go somewhere safe but unknown,' might help to make room for new challenges. We are looking here at a basic fear which most people will recognize; if there is more of a sense of basic security, people will be less fearful and will have more room for new challenges. It is the task of the manager or coach to re-establish a sense of security in the work situation. A secure work environment enables staff to be more flexible and offers the chance to break through counter-productive punctuation.

4.4 Content and context

Communication always takes place on two levels: on the level of *content* and on the level of *context*. Content refers to what is literally said, the message in the form of language; the context provides this with its meaning. The context reveals the nature of the relationship between the two parties and the relationship in its turn influences the message – the content. Both the coding and decoding of a message is affected by the context.

> Tom and Gerry work together. They trust each other and enjoy their working relationship. Gerry comes in one morning clearly feeling down. Tom says: 'Are you okay?' Gerry's eyes immediately fill with tears and she tells Tom that things are not going well at home and that she has slept very badly. He listens to her and after a while Gerry begins to feel a bit better. The atmosphere is relaxed.
>
> Steven and Gerry work together. When Gerry works with Steven she is always slightly on her guard; Steven is mostly more concerned with himself than with clients or colleagues. One morning Gerry seems not quite herself and Steven asks: 'Are you okay?' Gerry shrugs her shoulders and her reaction is non-committal; she has never had the feeling that Steven is really interested in her emotional welfare. A slight tension is left hanging in the air.

The relationship which these pairs of colleagues have with each other determines how the spoken message, in this case the same content in each of the examples: 'Are you okay?' is interpreted and responded to. The context gives colour to the content and influences the effect of the message.

The context is made up of the following aspects:
- The *relationship* which people have with one another: hierarchical, private, formal, friendly, intimate.
- The *tone* and *attitude* of both parties, for instance, open, closed, warm, humorous, nagging, attacking, hostile.
- The *intention* of the sender's *message*, is it for instance a request, an announcement, an order?
- The way in which the message is *received* and how the message is *interpreted* by the receiver: as a request, an announcement, an order?

To summarize: messages with their content are sent with a particular intention and are received in a particular way. This interaction of meanings is what forms the context and the context determines the colour and effect of the content.

Defining features in daily practice

As manager of a large company, Tim has the task of designing a new policy-document which must be implemented by middle-management in their various departments. All sorts of cost-cutting measures must be taken, there must be a reduction in the employment of agency staff and higher production targets have to be met. After each departmental manager has been informed of the plans in writing, a meeting is held during which the urgency of the new measures is emphasized and everyone is asked if the plans are clear. Tim expects a flourishing start to the new policy initiatives! In the following meeting there is a change in atmosphere. The management team is doing its best but is having to compromise between cutting costs and meeting production targets. Tim, up until now a supportive coach, has the feeling that he is having to justify his actions repeatedly and he starts to put the pressure on. Nobody is pleased with this radical change of atmosphere, which does nothing to promote co-operation within the team.
Tim takes this problem to his next session with his own coach. After some reflection they conclude that Tim has not been getting what he wants from his management team – results – and has reacted by pushing them harder. As the good coach he is, and from a position of trust in his team, he could have put questions to them, like: 'What are the factors that are making it difficult for you? Are the targets we have set realistic? I can see the effort you are putting in, is there any way in which I can help?'
Tim wasn't able to do this, because an feeling from the past got in the way. Tim had a mother who didn't see what his emotional needs were and at the same time knew how to put emotional pressure on him to make him behave as she wanted. His resistance to her took the form of emotional pressure from his side to get what *he* wanted, although this never got him what he really wanted: to be seen by her as the child he was.
In this stressful period of cutbacks, Tim temporarily reverts to an old pattern of behaviour. He has the feeling that he is not seen and acknowledged by his team and interprets their feelings of impotence as reluctance: he tries to counter this by exerting emotional pressure on them, behaviour which is coloured by both his mother's past example and his own accompanying feelings of impotence and anger. On the level of context, negative labeling on Tim's part: 'They don't value me enough to do what I ask of them… they don't see what I need… they're letting me down,' fails to act as an invitation to his team to co-operate (context), which means that the initiatives (content) cannot be implemented.

4.5 Closeness and distance

In every contact the concepts of *distance* and *closeness*, in other words the level of emotional involvement, play an important part. When we are dependent upon another person in some way, we feel instinctively and unerringly exactly how much distance the other is taking in relation to us and also whether this matches the distance or closeness we ourselves wish. Every situation has its own possibilities and its own limitations, its own wishes and conditions and its own closeness and distance. As a rule our contact with our GP usually feels closer than with our dentist, whilst the nature of the profession means that the dentist in fact has to perform very intimate actions. Every day we make many choices about how close we want to be to other people; on the bus, tram or underground many people prefer to stand rather than to sit next to someone they do not know; when we are sad we know instinctively who we want to have close by and who not. In each different work situation a different measure of professional distance is required and expected of us.

One supervisor or manager may feel closer and more accessible and another more distant and yet both are capable of offering adequate leadership qualities. A warm, emotionally-involved supervisor brings different but no less important qualities to bear on a situation from one who has strong organizational skills and maintains a more objective distance; when a supervisor or coach gets too close emotionally to the client for comfort, it can have a smothering effect. Dependent upon his or her transference and countertransference issues, one practitioner will be more or less sensitive to closeness and distance than another and practitioners who are able to manage their own boundaries well will be in a better position to judge distance and to be sensitive to signals in this area than those who have more difficulty with stating and setting boundaries.

Whenever a client enters a care setting, be it non-residential, semi-residential or residential, there is always an element of dependency in the relationship. It will certainly make a difference if the client is the recipient of voluntary or a compulsory care but ultimately all clients are dependent upon the care which is offered to them. The client presents with a care need and is the recipient of that care, the practitioner offers the care that is within the range of possibilities available. The quality of care is largely dependent upon the personal capacities of the caregiver.

Defining features in daily practice

> Some years ago Sacha's father died, suddenly and unexpectedly in the middle of the night. He was in his early seventies and she is his eldest daughter. When she arrived at hospital at seven in the morning, she was received by a male nurse who leaned towards her a little too closely with an expression of great sympathy and in a soft, extremely unctuous voice told her in a few muffled words that her father had departed this life: 'They were sadly unable to save him.' Almost immediately following this he asked her if the hospital had her permission to do an autopsy. The word was new to Sacha but it meant cutting her elderly father open. 'I don't think he would have wanted that,' said Sacha, after some thought. The nurse then said that they would be needing the bed very soon because they were extremely busy and they had left her father lying there for some hours whilst they waited for her to arrive – she had had to travel a considerable distance to get there. No doubt all these questions and comments were necessary and dictated by time-pressure and lack of space, but Sacha found the nurse's approach most distasteful. Despite her grief she was annoyed by the insincerity of the little performance which had greeted her and the abrupt and insensitive switch to the order of the day.
>
> A few years later, Sacha has to go into hospital herself for a major operation and she is received by a nurse with an easy, sympathetic manner. He sees her fear but also responds to her cynical jokes, realizing that they are her way of getting through the hours before the operation. Whilst explaining to her what is going to happen, the nurse sits at exactly the right distance from her, neither too close nor too far away. Sacha has second thoughts – she realizes just what an art it must be to be able to respond in exactly the right way to all those different patients with all their fears and all their off-jokes!

As a friend puts it: every nurse, social care practitioner, educator or counselor, manager, supervisor or coach needs to be equipped with a full palette of colours, in all tints and nuances, in order to respond with empathy and attunement to all sorts of people in all manner of situations, without forfeiting anything of his or her sincerity or authenticity. This is clearly asking a great deal!

Whilst the care worker needs to create an atmosphere of closeness, security and a certain degree of intimacy, at the same time s/he must maintain a professional distance. This might seem like a contradiction in terms and yet it can be done; finding the right balance in this typifies the quality of the guidance and care. With every client and in every new situation the worker will have to assess and reassess what is being asked of him or her: professional closeness or professional distance – and the closeness is defined by the professional distance. We could say that in the course of continuous interaction every worker needs to keep making decisions about the appropriate physical and emotional distance s/he needs to observe and sometimes also needs to keep under careful watch.

> Jennifer has a job as a prison officer and works in a detention centre. She likes to be seen as a sort of mother-figure by the male detainees and the quality of her contact with most of them is good. They trust her, she spends a lot of time with them in their cells listening as 'her lads' unburden themselves to her. This behaviour can sometimes put her in a tight corner, because she finds it difficult to set clear limits: a detainee had recently put on a porn film whilst she was still in his cell. At that moment she hadn't known how to react and had just got up and left the cell, but walked round afterwards in a fury about it and had subsequently avoided the man without giving him any explanation.
> During her upbringing Jennifer has learned that as a woman she should always put others first. She says that she enjoys giving attention to other people, but she also says that she has great difficulty in setting limits in case she hurts someone's feelings. In fact she is scared that other people will reject *her* or not like her any more if she asserts her boundaries or says no and it is for this reason that she sometimes gives her clients too much leeway. This arises out of an old feeling: transference. If as a child she stuck up for herself or didn't want to look after her brothers because she thought that they should clear up after themselves, she got: 'That's not what nice little girls say', from her father, or later: 'Call yourself a woman?'
> In the end the situation gets out of hand because she doesn't make things clear: close and caring one minute, distant and aloof the next; then she gets furious with the other person because he crossed a boundary which she had not made clear in the first place: countertransference.

> Jennifer is pleased with the contact she has with Carlos, one of the detainees. He is inside for assault and is badly scarred from the burns he received when his ex-wife threw hot fat over him during a fight. There followed years of rage during which he held women completely at bay and Jennifer is probably the first woman whom Carlos has allowed himself to trust again. They spend a lot of time talking together. One day Jennifer is sitting in the common room in the company of some colleagues and some of the other detainees; Carlos sees that Jennifer is tired and he offers to massage her shoulders. Jennifer rebuffs his offer – she thinks he is going too far, particularly here in front of her colleagues. Carlos flies into a rage and spits at her; as a result of this behaviour he is transferred to another detention centre.
>
> Carlos's fury undoubtedly has to do with the fact that he has been able to transfer onto Jennifer an old need to be cared for, a need which she has met and for which he would like to give something back, something out of his own caring-reservoir. His intention is rejected and this in front of other prison officers and fellow detainees. The misunderstood child in him is so enraged by this humiliation that he literally spits out his fury. Jennifer's countertransference also contributes to the fact that things escalated so quickly; she should have maintained a more professional distance in relation to this detainee: because of her own difficulty in saying 'no' she 'had to' react tactlessly when this unexpected situation arose. We could say that this is a case in which transference and countertransference go completely hand-in-glove.

4.6 Dependency

As we have seen, the dependency which is characteristic of so many working relationships provides a fruitful breeding ground for both positive and negative transference; both parties are involved in a continuous process of interaction and interdependency, even if they do not always experience this as such. In any team, the members are dependent upon their colleagues for a productive working relationship. Managers are dependent for co-operation and productivity upon their staff, workers are and feel dependent upon their managers, supervisors or coaches for evaluation of their performance. Students are dependent for the assessment of their progress upon their lecturers who in their turn are dependent upon the efforts and application of their students. Clients are and feel dependent upon the quality of the care and attention offered to them by therapists, social care practitioners or counselors, who can only give effective support if their clients allow them to do so. Someone who has committed an offence is dependent upon the police officer, who is in turn dependent upon the offender for a confession. People who are admitted to hospital feel dependent upon the time and care which the medical and nursing staff are able and willing to give them, and must then co-operate with staff by accepting the care necessary for their recovery.

> Judy was born in Suriname. Shortly after her birth, Judy's father died and her mother gave her away to an aunt, whom Judy called her foster-mother and who took Judy back to the Netherlands with her. This aunt had other children and Judy was just one too many; she could never do anything right. Her birth mother never showed any interest in her and when Judy, now twenty-eight and with children of her own, finally went over to visit her, her mother just turned to Judy and asked her what she was doing there: 'Isn't it bad enough that I had to lose my husband after you were born?' In her mother's eyes, Judy, then a tiny baby of a few weeks old, was personally responsible for her father's death.
>
> Judy is following a vocational training in social care work; she is intelligent enough but her attendance is poor and when she comes to college she is so tired that she can hardly keep her eyes open. Her tutor, who likes Judy but who has heard just too many excuses from her – she didn't hear the alarm clock, there was a power-cut on the underground, she's pregnant again – confronts her about her attendance, saying that she is now really starting to put her training on the line.
>
> During a subsequent conversation Judith tells her mentor that she is scared of her and has nightmares about her. 'What do I do? Do I hit you, do I scream at you, do I send you away?' asks the mentor. 'No, nothing like that. I think you're very nice and I always tell everybody what a great mentor you are and how I really trust you, and still I'm dead scared of you, even though I know there's no need to be. I really want you to like me and that's when I end up coming late and then I just get into a complete panic.'

> Judy projects onto her female mentor, who is about the same age as her mother and her aunt, the expectation that she will be rejected, not for her behaviour but for herself as a person. This is an old feeling, an old fear arising out of an old reality: transference. In fact Judy herself evokes rejection with her current behaviour and thereby recreates for herself the old, familiar reality of being rejected. Rationally, Judy knows that the mentor has every reason to confront her, as part of the job of guiding her towards her goal of becoming a qualified social care worker, but emotionally Judy becomes totally blocked in her presence. In relationship to authority Judy feels so completely dependent upon the good will of the other that she is on constant high alert for the tiniest sign of disapproval; because of this she loses touch with her sense of reality and gets into even deeper trouble. Inside her there is an exhausting but unremitting battle between her Vulnerable Child and her Critical Parent.

Because authority is a feature of many working relationships, particularly within education and social care, this can mean that for some people feelings of dependency will be magnified. Because of the nature of the working relationship and this aspect of it, it can sometimes be very difficult for the practitioner – the authority – to break through the transference process.

> Sara, a young woman of twenty-eight, is in therapy. She is the daughter of an aloof, rejecting, demanding mother and a reasonably kind but largely absent father. In her mother eyes, nothing that Sara did was ever good enough. Sara is a singer and gives singing lessons for a living. 'You could do so much better for yourself than this,' her mother says. None of her boyfriends ever comes up to scratch either: 'Sara deserves better than this one.' In saying this her mother manages to reject not only the boyfriend but also Sara's choice.
> Sara is insecure and chaotic and is finally trying to get her life back on track. During a session Sara tells her therapist about her boyfriend and how he brings her breakfast in bed and massages her shoulders when she's tense, but also that he works much too hard and sometimes drinks

too much. The therapist questions her further about her relationship with this boyfriend: does Sara get what she needs from her partner? What sort of changes would she like to see in the relationship?

A few days after this session Sara meets a friend and tells her angrily and with a slight edge of despair that her therapist has told her to leave her boyfriend. She is already planning how she's going to tell him. This friend, who also knows Sara and her boyfriend as a couple, can't understand this at all. As far as she can see, they have a good relationship. 'Talk to your therapist again before you do anything rash,' says her friend.

When Sara arrives for her next appointment, her therapist can see that she is holding onto a lot of rage. She invites Sara to express her anger and Sara tells her that 'she's got a nerve, trying to tell her that her boyfriend isn't good enough and that she's had it up to here with all that rejection stuff!' Sara transfers onto her therapist the belief that she rejects her boyfriend, something which her therapist in fact did not do; all she did was to ask some questions about the relationship and how Sara would like it to be. Sara's mother, on the other hand, always was and still is critical of her choices. Sara listened to her mother when she was young and obeyed her too, even though she didn't want to, because she was afraid of losing her love. Now she has the tendency to listen to her therapist in the same way and she hears her therapist saying things which her mother used to say. The difference is that in the end she doesn't actually do what she thinks her therapist has told her to do, but she does transfer the old pent-up anger which she felt towards her mother onto her therapist. Sara is dependent on other people for esteem, care and the right to exist and this also makes her angry. If this transference can be named and recognized, it will eventually lead to insight, relief and greater independence.

To summarize, it can be said that the social care practitioner is expected to have the ability to:
- recognize and acknowledge resistance
- manage resistance adequately
- recognize transference issues for what they are
- respond appropriately to transference issues
- help clients or co-workers to make productive use of transference issues

- recognize and acknowledge countertransference issues
- manage countertransference issues adequately

In the next chapter we shall make some links between the concepts of transference and countertransference and the professional skills and standards of good practice which the practitioner is expected to possess. We shall make use of examples of how these skills are applied in daily practice to further clarify the role played by transference and more especially by countertransference. Making use of questions, comments and a few detailed examples, we shall invite readers to reflect upon their own qualities and how they can best apply them in their daily work: what are their strengths, what are their limitations and where do their own countertransference issues lurk?

The professional conduct and skills of the practitioner 5

Transference and countertransference in practice

There are certain qualities and skills which for a therapist, a supervisor, a coach or a manager are a prerequisite for effective work in the care sector and are necessary in order to lay the foundations for a functional and productive relationship with a client or a co-worker. Qualities, convictions, beliefs, values and norms together form the basic attitude or the frame of reference within which we operate. We test our behaviour constantly against this frame of reference, which we have formed over the years as a result of our natural aptitude and temperament, our upbringing and our experience and which hopefully we have subjected to continual adjustment. From these basic materials we develops our skills as practitioners and where necessary refine and add to them.

Productive care workers are people who can act as a stimulus to processes of change and can guide them. They possess the qualities of respect, acceptance, empathy and positive openness and can also confront and offer feedback in a skilful way. In addition to this it is important that they enjoy the work they do, can keep things in proportion, have a sense of humour and are genuinely interested in the people for and with whom they work.

It is to be hoped that a tiler enjoys laying tiles, a baker likes making bread and a taxi-driver takes pleasure in driving because this will increase the quality of their product. Similarly, we may hope that a manager aspires to good leadership and coaching skills, that a therapist, counselor or supervisor actively likes other people and their particularities, that a care worker takes pleasure in offering good quality care and that an officer in the prison service finds it a challenge to work with confined and often aggressive clients.

It is important for all professionals to get something out of what they do and to take pleasure in their work. Working with people is sometimes seen as a vocation and one which brings its own rewards, as though a worker in the 'people professions' only has to give unstintingly out of a bottomless well of human charity and will get gratitude in return. This is not the case and neither should it be. Of course, a certain measure of idealism plays a part in such a career-choice and the sense of a 'calling' is fine in its way, but the most important thing is that those of us who choose to work with people have the creativity to make the work enjoyable and to keep it that way and also are able to enjoy the person or persons with whom they work; this asks for real curiosity, a sense of proportion and a sense of humour. A productive practitioner is enthusiastic but discerning, can show patience but also get annoyed, makes mistakes and can also acknowledge them, has an inquiring mind but can also let go of work, is constantly developing and also knows how to relax.

5.1 Transference? Countertransference?

The theme transference and countertransference are so central to this book that the reader could be forgiven for assuming that almost everything that happens between people on a feeling level could be classified as having something to do with transference and countertransference issues. Whilst this *may* be so it does not necessarily *have* to be. Any attempt to attribute all feelings, pleasant and unpleasant, to transference would not only be time-consuming but also not particularly useful. Ordinary feelings of affection or annoyance exist, need to exist and in fact are essential to any functional interaction because these feelings say something about the relationship and the people involved in it. It is sometimes useful to name the feeling that a person evokes in us and to offer feedback about it, and at other times it is not. Telling other people that we really like them can be functional if it serves a particular purpose: lightening the atmosphere, working towards improving the other's self-image, clarifying the relationship, or even just being spontaneous. But the real point here is that not everything always needs to be said, in professional relationships as well in personal ones.

Similarly, telling other people that we feel annoyed by them can have its function if the irritation is getting in the way of productive contact. It can be equally useful to speak about such feelings if the person in question evokes irritation in a number of other people as well, but has up until now never been confronted with this because it has not been adequately mirrored back; in effect the others have withheld the feedback which might enable him or her to adjust the annoying behaviour. But let's say we are annoyed by a client or colleague because we came to work already tired and irritable so that our perceptions are not altogether unclouded, or if the annoyance is about something insignificant or something which the client can do nothing about, then naming the irritation could easily influence the relationship negatively rather than positively. In other words it does not always need to be said!

So when is a feeling 'just there' and when is it a sign of transference and countertransference? The answer to this question can only be found through conscious self-reflection, by evaluating and daring to look critically at our ways of communicating and interacting, through experience and by asking for advice and feedback, for example: 'I had a confrontation with… this afternoon and I feel uneasy about it. Do you have time to listen?' An attentive ear and some careful questions from a colleague can often help to clarify a situation.

Sometimes the intensity of the feeling which another person evokes in us can point us towards possible transference issues. On the other hand, there are people who just happen to evoke strong feelings of tenderness, sensuality, distance, closeness, resistance or irritation in us because of their appearance, their charisma or their behaviour. Provided they are perceived consciously, these feelings can offer certain indicators within the interaction, but they are not *necessarily* transference and countertransference.

5.1.1 An attempt at clarification

A client or worker often arrives late and this is beginning to cause feelings of annoyance and exasperation. The subject is addressed, the feelings of irritation are perhaps mentioned and the client or worker can be firmly requested to come on time in future; end of story.

If despite this, the client or worker's habit of turning up late persists, some other action may be needed in the form of dismissal or ending the contact, but it may also be helpful to look at some very telling transference issues. For instance:

- The client is afraid of and/or angry with authority figures and always

turns up late because of resistance; the client dares neither to speak about this nor to cancel the appointment.
- The client is so nervous and tense about being late that something always goes wrong.
- The client has never been brought into line by those who brought him or her up and is waiting to be given clear boundaries.

If there is indeed a question of transference, bringing this out into the open and talking about it can help the client to become more conscious of underlying feelings, which in turn can form the first step in the process of becoming more skilled in managing them; this insight into what motivates the persistent lateness can be helpful to the client in both the professional and the personal sphere.

There could be a case of countertransference here, too, if the practitioner, manager, supervisor or coach:
- feels personally rejected by the client's persistent late arrival
- does not dare to state boundaries or give feedback in relation to the client's late arrival

The practitioner could take the intensity of the feelings – extreme irritation, disappointment or a feeling of powerlessness – as a warning that a countertransference issue is lurking and could bring this feeling, or the situation in which it arises, into his or her own supervision or coaching session.

It is fine for a client or worker to evoke a feeling of strong affection and appreciation in a practitioner, supervisor or coach, provided that this has a positive effect on the worker. It is very pleasant to feel at ease and secure in another person's company and it is also pleasant to be appreciated – these feelings contribute greatly to good working relationships and need provide no cause for concern. There may, however, be a question of transference which may need to be addressed, if for instance:
- the client does not enter into or maintain other contacts because s/he feels sufficiently nourished within the contact with the practitioner not to need them
- the client places the practitioner on a pedestal and continues to do so in a disproportionate way

- the client falls in love with the practitioner and shows no signs of getting over it

There may be a question of countertransference if practitioners, supervisors or coaches:
- behave in a way which strengthens or fosters feelings of love in the client
- can only work with clients who put them on a pedestal
- like to see themselves as indispensable and foster this feeling in their client because they themselves need the admiration and appreciation which goes with being irreplaceable

5.2 (Self)knowledge, (self)consciousness and (self)reflection

Thinking about feelings and behaviour, evaluating behaviour and talking to a colleague or colleagues, a coach or supervisor about our own actions and interventions, gives us insight into our own conduct. What is perhaps even more important is opening ourselves to feelings, our own and other people's, and allowing ourselves to experience what is happening, in ourselves and in the other person. The next and vital step is to work out what to do with our experience, to find the language to help us make clear to others what we perceive about ourselves and about them and to use questions and feedback in such a way that others do not experience themselves as being rejected or criticized but instead feel invited to join us in thinking about what is going on. This applies to all parties, client and practitioner, co-worker and manager.

As practitioners we must be willing:
- to *experience* what is happening to us on a feeling level
- to have the courage to look at this *critically*
- if necessary to discuss this self-reflection with our colleague
- to use our transference feelings in a productive way
- to name the other person's transference

Here follows an example of how to recognize and deal with transference:

> Ten students, on a day-release vocational training course and all between the ages of twenty and forty-five, have at the end of their college day a group supervision, led by one of their lecturers. At the beginning of the session this lecturer, Hanna, always asks the students how their day has been. A few of them say they were pleased with the day, but then suddenly one of the students, Doreen, says: 'It was a boring old load of long-winded rambling. Your class was just about okay but the rest of it- we just seemed to be going round in circles – all that endless repetition...'. Hanna notices that Doreen's remarks and more particularly her denigrating tone, have quite an impact on her. Hanna looks round at the others; all eyes are turned expectantly on her. 'I shall have to do something with this,' thinks Hanna. Doreen adopts this tone in class quite often, and it is not an inviting one, in fact it feels hostile. Hanna says to Doreen: 'You know it's okay for you to be critical of the course, it's just that the way you say it doesn't give me the feeling that I can have an open discussion with you about it. How do the others feel about this?' The other students confirm that they have difficulty with Doreen's remarks. 'Is it okay with you if we go into this a bit further?' Hanna asks Doreen. Doreen blushes; she is a bit shocked by the effect of her comments. 'Yes, sure,' says Doreen, who is also disarmingly honest. 'I'd like to look at it, because I often seem to get it wrong.'
> So the lecturer and the other students ask Doreen some questions:
> - Is it that you just want to express your dissatisfaction?
> - Do you want to give us the feeling that we're slow learners?
> - What kind of effect do you want to achieve with your comments?
> - Where does your dissatisfaction come from?
> - How would you like things to change and what could you do to make this happen?

In the course of this discussion it emerges that Doreen had an extremely demanding father who spoke to her in exactly the same tone she now uses towards her lecturer and fellow students in the supervision group. Doreen always felt that in her father's eyes she was a failure. Everything she did had to be 'worthwhile' and had to be done quickly and efficiently; nothing she did was ever good enough and she never had the feeling that she was okay as she was. It made her very sad at the time and talking about it now it makes her sad all over again. She sometimes projects her feeling of failure onto others by making her annoyance abundantly clear, but in the end she is the one who has the most trouble with this feeling. Because she is unable to enjoy anything which does not appear to have an immediate practical use, she feels compelled to make her discomfort immediately and clearly visible and this has the effect of alienating other people instead of inviting them to give her their support or understanding.

By letting Doreen know what kind of feelings her behaviour evokes in other people and by giving her feedback and to some extent confronting her, her fellow students invite her to become more aware of the effect of her behaviour and to reflect upon it, to share it and to experience it more fully. In this way she can begin to work through it.

In the following example, Ellen becomes conscious of her countertransference issue with her client and starts to deal with it:

> Ellen works in the rehabilitation unit of a large residential centre for people with a mental disablility. In her role as mentor she has just had a new client assigned to her, Elspeth, who is paralyzed down one side following a brain hemorrhage. Her prognosis is reasonably good. She is a youthful woman in her sixties, fifteen or so years older than Ellen, and during their first conversation Elspeth tells Ellen about her life, her education, her work and her divorce, which happened more than twenty years ago. She talks about how, without any warning, her husband suddenly ran off with one of her best friends, and this whilst they had always had such an incredibly good marriage! She talks about her grown-up children who hardly ever come to visit her. She says with some indignation that here at the centre she feels excluded by the other residents on the unit.
> It becomes clear in the course of the conversation that Elspeth feels that everything in her life happens to her as the result of some fatal coincidence in which she apparently plays no part.
> When Ellen gently tries to ask her what her own part in these various situations might have been, Elspeth reacts in a supercilious, offended and irritable way. Ellen begins to ask some open questions but soon starts to feel as if she is being too insistent and that her questioning is having an

adverse effect; she can feel the tension and is unable to break it.

When the conversation is over, Ellen experiences a great sense of relief and it feels as though a knot in her stomach is slowly unraveling. Later, thinking about the conversation and wondering what it is about Elspeth that bothers her so much, Ellen begins to realize that the intensity of her reaction must almost certainly have something to do with *her*. After all, Elspeth's response wasn't *that* bad! Back at home Ellen decides to get to the bottom of it. At college she has had classes about this sort of confrontation; she starts to leaf through one of her textbooks and yes, there it is: this seems to point to an old feeling and it's called transference and if you're the practitioner, it's called countertransference. So, what does this intense feeling remind her of, and who or what gave her and maybe still gives her, a knot in her stomach?

'My mother of course!' Ellen suddenly realizes. When she was a child, Ellen's mother was extremely egocentric and completely unable to put herself in another person's place. Her mother's emotions provided the norm for what the rest of the family were supposed to feel. One of the unwritten rules was: sadness was allowed, anger wasn't. The children had to apologize regularly for what they usually felt to be justified anger, but the parents never apologized for their own self-centred, often unreasonable behaviour. Whatever went wrong in the family was never the mother's fault and she wouldn't allow any discussion about her conduct. If, in the face of this, her husband or children ever tried to give her some feedback, she immediately made a convincing display of being deeply hurt, sad and misunderstood. Ellen then had the feeling that she had give her mother sympathy and comfort, whilst of course it was her mother who should have been comforting her. At moments like this Ellen got a terrible knot in her stomach, a tight bundle of powerlessness and anger.

Elspeth's lofty, slightly injured air, in combination with Ellen's susceptibility to this kind of attitude, evokes in Ellen her childhood feelings of powerlessness and anger, the anger which wasn't allowed. This is not a very useful feeling to take into a new counselling process.

Ellen could make a choice out of several options here:
- She could tell Elspeth that this countertransference issue makes it inadvisable for her to counsel her and that a colleague will be taking over from her.

- She could use her new insight to be a better guide for Elspeth from now on: she can take a deep breath and listen respectfully and with a certain professional distance to her story, and if possible help her, with some caution, to look at the role she takes in relation to the rest of the group.
- She could try to give words to Elspeth's behaviour and perhaps at a later stage in the contact speak to her about the countertransference feelings she has herself experienced. This could serve to facilitate the process of learning about and coming to terms with these issues for both of them.

It is almost impossible to offer definitive guidelines about how to recognize transference issues and, having once become conscious of these, how to deal with them in a professional way. Being alert to body language can be useful, as can remaining open to our own feelings; what can be particularly helpful is sitting back every now and then, taking a bit of distance from the situation and asking ourselves the simple question: What is happening now?

For example:
- I keep asking the same question, each time in a slightly different way, and I'm not getting an answer.
- I have the feeling that I'm working harder all the time whilst the other person is doing less.
- I have feelings of irritations but try to suppress them.
- I have feelings of irritation; I notice that I'm being a bit abrupt and that my tone isn't right.
- I find this client so sweet and so vulnerable that I don't say what I think.
- I find this worker so intimidating that I don't say what I think.
- I'm nearly falling asleep, I'm bored. How can I bring more action into this conversation?

We could think of countless situations in which it is helpful to take time to reflect on what is actually going on and to ask ourselves: What can I do with this? How can I make this feeling serve the situation? If we keep on working too hard or asking the same question in a different form, we stay on the level of content and do not come a step further. One way of breaking out of this circle is to say to the client or co-worker: 'I notice that I keep thinking of new questions and that you give me answers to them, but I have the feeling that we are not really reaching each other. Do you have that feeling too?' In this way we invite the other person to become actively involved in the conversation. Or we can say: 'Somehow or other I'm a little bit wary of you. Do you think I need to be?' or 'Is that what you want?' On the level of context the other person is then invited to take joint responsibility for a feeling which may not have been transmitted consciously, but which nevertheless has been received.

Self-knowledge, self-consciousness, self-reflection and communication skills are all necessary for work at a professional level in social care. We shall now look at some of the specific qualities which professional practitioners who are engaged in intensive contact with others need to make their own. By each of the qualities there will be a short explanation of the term followed by an analysis of some examples of transference and countertransference. Whilst reading each paragraph, it might be useful to ask ourselves some questions: What place does respect hold in my work? Where do my boundaries lie? Am I okay with this or is there something here I need to learn? Am I open enough towards my clients? Where do the limits of my empathy lie and what happens when I reach them? Do I know how to speak about my feelings in a 'fruitful' way, do I invite co-operation and, where needed, change? Can I manage confrontation, can I find the words for what I want to say or am I afraid of hurting the other person or of not being liked?

5.3 Respect

What we mean here by respect is: taking the other person seriously. This has nothing to do with the deference which comes from holding the other in high regard or fearing the other, as some dictionaries would have it, but: 'doing to the other as you would be done by'. It is the willingness to allow the other truly to be 'the other', with other feelings, other convictions, other values and other ways of behaving from our own. This does not imply that the practitioner necessarily has to condone the other person's behaviour, it only says that the practitioner should attempt to recognize and understand this behaviour in relation to the other's background, circumstances and current situation.

The quality of respect should be part of every practitioner's basic 'equipment', but not necessarily in equal measure and of course every practitioner will have a different interpretation of what respectful behaviour is. These differences do not necessarily mean that a particular worker is more or less suited for the job, but what does make a difference is if the worker is able draw upon reserves of respect which s/he has received in the past. Giving respect to others is made easier by having received a generous measure of it oneself, but this is not to say that those of us who have had too little respect paid to us in our early years are unable to come up with it as adults. Generally speaking what it will ask of us is a period of self-exploration during which we to some extent come to terms with our own sense of rejection.

> Rascha, who in an earlier example says to David, aged two-and-a-half: 'It is not up to you,' shows him no respect. She does not respect him in his 'otherness' as a little boy who is just beginning to discover his own will. *She finds him* lacking in respect because he doesn't listen. Obedience is for her a value which up until now has gone unquestioned: *this* is how you show respect to those older than yourself. As a small child she was shown no respect: she was never asked what she wanted or how she felt. You have to listen to those in authority, that's just how it is, but this doesn't stop it being painful. The small child in Rascha wants to get some respect at last and she tries to get it from David. She transfers an old feeling onto him – countertransference – and as a result of this is unable to treat him with respect.

If Rascha wants to be a professional child care worker, she will need to gain insight into the way in which she tries to get respect from children. Only then, when she has become fully aware of this, will she be able to give the children the guidance they really need from her.

> Ivy, a practitioner of around forty, has since recently been working with adults with an intellectual disability. Her colleagues say that she does too much for the residents; she ties shoe-laces, makes sandwiches for them and fastens coats if a resident is struggling with buttons and buttonholes. Her colleagues say that she must show more respect for her clients' abilities and must encourage them to do things for themselves. Ivy, on the other hand, sees the residents as children, because that's how things were seen in the home she came from. She had a younger sister with an intellectual disability whom everybody had to make allowances for all the time, simply because she had a disability. This has formed Ivy's frame of reference. As a small child from a large family, Ivy had to learn to be independent very quickly; there was no room for being cared for. You had to look after your younger brothers and sisters and grow up as quickly as possible so as to be less of a burden to your parents. As a child Ivy yearned for care and attention and she bestows her childhood need onto the residents lavishly; she wants to give them as much as she can. Her colleagues consider this as transgressing her clients' boundaries and as disrespectful. Ivy finds it extremely difficult not to take care of other people, partly because if she lets her clients do everything for themselves, she feels as though she is not 'working'. She gains affirmation for herself by taking care of other people; at home this was the only way in which she could get affirmation and it made her 'important'. This countertransference makes it difficult for Ivy to let go of her 'taking care of' role; she needs to experience that she has worth even if she doesn't look after other people. She will need to discover and to value the fact that she has other good qualities apart from her ability to 'take care of'. Only when she can to give herself this acknowledgement will she be able to let go of her hold on this single, central role.

When do we call behaviour respectful and when not? The most objective criterion might be: the client's experience. In the previous example it is by no means certain whether the residents see Ivy's rather patronizing behaviour as showing lack of respect; they may well find it rather convenient. The notion of *respect* needs not only to match the convictions of the practitioner or the client, but to fit into a wider social view on the concept of care.

5.3.1 Limits and respect

We all have limits on our capacity for respect, a point at which we cease to be sympathetic. We sometimes reach this because we simply stop wanting to be sympathetic, sometimes because emotionally we can no longer sustain it. In general terms it is only human to have these limits on our respect and it is not always inevitable that we fail the person in question; we can often simply avoid this person. In work situations however it is important that we are conscious of these limits and can look critically at them. 'Why am I unsympathetic towards this client? How come I'm unable to come up with any understanding for this person? Why do I have the feeling that I only want to correct this client, why does s/he drive me up the wall, why do I want to reject him or her, why do I not intervene if s/he is humiliated by other clients. Am I failing my client? How can I put my lack of respect to some kind of professional use?'

Adults who as children were able to express their thoughts and feelings are generally kinder in their judgments of other people than those who experienced rejection of their feelings and their behaviour as children. Adults who felt acknowledged and accepted in all their many different feelings are likely to be able to enter more easily into intimate relationships with others and often have a relatively mild and subtle way of looking at male-female roles, sexual inclination and religious beliefs and are likely to be more tolerant of behaviour which deviates from the norm. Generally speaking, qualities like good-natured humour and the ability to put things into perspective are the benchmarks of a respectful practitioner.
A noticeable and strong tendency to be rejecting of divergent behaviour, rigid standards, demeaning or sexually-tinted humour along with the urge to punish, often characterize adults who have trouble with intimacy, who are attached to power and order and who have never dared or been able to express a whole range of feelings, particularly those of powerlessness and fear. We could say that people who have experienced lack of intimacy in their childhood have a great deal of difficulty in finding it in later life; the possibility exists that they will unwittingly and unintentionally, damage others in their turn.

In society in general, people tend to react with the strongest outrage to issues which concern children: the fate of children in war zones, the physical, mental and sexual abuse of children or their neglect. A child's distress evokes more emotion in most adults than anything else. Many workers in the prison service have extreme difficulty with pedophiles and those who have committed incest, as if these offences would be top of the hierarchy of crimes, were one to exist. For most people this is where the boundary to their respect lies: these offences exceed the limits of any understanding. Generally speaking people have more difficulty with a pedophile than with a perpetrator of street-crime involving a fatality, more trouble with someone who has committed incest than with a drunken taxi-driver who has run over and killed a child. Residents in a local community are more likely to start a witch hunt against a suspected pedophile than against a suspected perpetrator of violent crime.

Many people are able to avoid this deeply-rooted feeling of aversion towards pedophiles because they seldom or never come into contact with the offender. This is not the case for those who work in social care, psychiatric care or the judiciary; they cannot always keep out of the way of particular individuals and can therefore be confronted with the boundaries of their own respect.

It may be possible that it is those people who have carefully concealed their hurt and their own feelings of powerlessness behind strongly judgmental thoughts and feelings, who find deviant behaviour such as pedophilia so confronting, emerging itself as it almost always does from a background of powerlessness and neglect. The contemplation of so much powerlessness, in both victim and perpetrator, would be too much to bear.

> Carlo, who works in a detention centre, is a man with a strong need for rules, order and discipline; he has very little belief in people's capacity for self-direction. In his view, avoiding punishment is for everybody a far stronger guiding principle than conscience. Even as a child this was in his opinion the only way to learn: none of this talk, just give them a good belting, he's done all right on it, hasn't he?… And anyway, he talks to his own kids, doesn't he? If they don't do their best at school he sits them down and gives them a good talking to. He tells them they're no good now and if they go on like this, nothing good will ever come of them either. And ac-

cording to Carlo it works, because afterwards they always do their best, at least for a few days. And he wouldn't have minded more pocket money and a red bike himself, but he hasn't turned into a child-rapist, has he? Well then! So you think I should I start understanding a man like that? They should hang them from the ceiling by their balls, that'll teach them! Carlo knows that as a worker he is expected to maintain a formal correctness in his treatment of detainees, but no more should be expected of him than that.

As a little boy of three Carlo landed in a children's home after his father went out for a breath of fresh air and never came back and his mother could no longer take care of him. It was nice and quiet there in that home. A few years later his mother came to fetch him, with a new stepfather, that's life, it didn't make him start thieving, did it? So there's no need for anybody else to go using that sort of thing as an argument. Talking about feelings is a waste of time. If his colleagues on the unit start doing this, he lets them know in no uncertain terms by the expression on his face that they are doing him no favours. The atmosphere always drops a few degrees when Carlo walks in.

Carlo's unconscious basic feeling is one of fear; he is afraid of the emotions which emerge if he loses control and this is the source of his transference and countertransference. If he were to respect other people's emotions, particularly the emotions which have to do with the experience of extreme powerlessness, he would be able to come closer to his own emotions. He avoids emotions and he has doubts about the integrity and professionalism of his colleagues who approach and discuss them. Unconsciously he is angry about the denial of his feelings and afraid of acknowledging the child in himself and thereby feeling his grief and his feelings of powerlessness as a child of three who was unable to do anything to change what was happening to him. Carlo is certainly capable of conducting himself in a correct manner, particularly in other people's eyes. What he is not capable of, and probably never will be unless he goes into therapy and dares to experience how it really was, is feeling and showing real respect, not for his colleagues, not for his clients and not for himself.

5.4 Acceptance

Acceptance, in the context of good practice, means being able to 'receive' other people as they are whilst not necessarily condoning all of their behaviour. Unconditional acceptance was seen by Carl Rogers, one of the founders of humanistic psychology, as a prerequisite for healthy development in the sense that children should not have to exist according to a set of pre-conditions but should allowed to be as they are, in all their capriciousness and unpredictability as well as in their more endearing qualities. A child is not rejected as a person if s/he is angry; the child is taught not to hurt himself or others in his rage, but s/he also learns that it is okay to be angry and this is what makes the difference. Caregivers guide children towards adulthood by offering them choices in the ways they behave; through the experience of being accepted by others children learn to accept themselves. This self-acceptance in turn enables them to be accepting of other people. We learn by mirroring and being mirrored: if other people listen to us, they mirror back to us that we are worth listening to. If other people laugh at our jokes we experience that, at that moment at least, we are funny and this gives us as pleasurable feeling and invites us to say something else that will make them laugh.

Many counselors or coaches will have had first-hand experience of how hard it is to counsel someone they really dislike, someone in whom they can find nothing appealing at all. This is a real struggle: hard work, heavy going and an extremely unattractive proposition for both parties. The counselor's initial task in a situation like this is to accept that s/he has these feelings in relation to the client or co-worker. Later on, in a supervision or coaching session, the counselor can always try to discover what it is that makes it so hard to accept the other person. Is it a question of countertransference? What exactly, in concrete behavioural terms, does the aversion consist of? If we can gain insight into our own contribution to a particular problem, be aware of any possible countertransference issues and combine our insight with an attitude of acceptance and a certain skill in naming concrete behaviour and re-framing this in the form of a request, it must surely be possible to improve any working relationship.

Marion is twenty-seven and has been working for several months at a centre for children with behavioural difficulties. Children stay there for varying periods of time, from several months to several years. Marion enjoys her work and is very good with the children; she seems to have an unerring sense of what they need. She is often the only one on her team who is able to make contact with the most withdrawn and closed-off children. By contrast, her contact with the parents is less successful. If parents ask questions about their child or have comments about how things are done at the centre, Marion experiences a strong feeling of anger rising up in her: 'They should have taken better care of their children', or 'They shouldn't have sent their children away from home, should they?' She is unable to come up with any understanding at all for the parents' circumstances or what might have led to their current inability to bring up their children themselves. She cannot accept their 'choice' to place their children in an institution and this blocks any co-operation; it also means that she cannot take part in the programme of regular contact with the parents. When her colleagues try to speak to her about this, they come up against the same block.

When Marion was still a toddler and for reasons which have never been explained to her, she was taken away from her home and placed in an institution. She has never been able to accept this and therefore cannot work it through. The damaged child in her contaminates, as it were, the adult, professional part. She transfers the rage which she still feels in relation to her own parents onto what she sees as failing parents in general: countertransference. If Marion wants to work with parents she will first have to accept her own history and her own parents' failure. Being able to accept that parents make mistakes, that her parents were apparently unable to take care of her and that this knowledge is painful will be key to her ability to change. Working through her grief includes being able to acknowledge on a feeling level that these parents who sent their children away from home are not *her* parents and therefore do not deserve her rejection.

Allison works as a management consultant and coach. Her client Richard is the manager of a university department. During a coaching session, Richard tells her about a conflict that he has had this week with a member of staff about his job description. The conflict had got out of hand; the staff member had become incensed with Richard and had flung a variety of reproaches at his head. This had affected Richard deeply and the conversation had ended badly. The following day the staff member had come to Richard with an apology but Richard had felt too hurt to accept it.

Allison notices that she starts to feel blocked when Richard says that he is unable to accept the sincerely-proffered apology. She feels a powerful irritation welling up and can no longer listen openly to what Richard is saying. She can hear the sound of rejection in her own tone when she responds to him but can do nothing to stop it; she feels the tension rising between herself and Richard, but she can no longer steer clear of it. She brings the conversation to a close with a strong feeling of dissatisfaction.

Allison is allergic to victim behaviour: 'people who walk around looking injured'. She has trouble with people who cry when, objectively speaking, there is really nothing to cry about. She cannot cope with people who, as she sees it, make a display of their hurt feelings.

Allison had a mother who spent years mourning the sudden death of her husband, Allison's father. When Annie reached adolescence she wasn't able to enter the normal teenage battles with her mother: it is very hard to fight with a grieving parent. Her mother never got angry, but instead was often hurt, sad and silent. Annie became a victim of her mother's victim behaviour, behaviour which made her feel powerless and saddled her with guilt feelings so that for years she had to swallow her anger. This anger comes out now, in the form of countertransference.

That evening Allison turns the conversation over in her mind and begins to realize where her irritation is coming from. In the next session she'll try to respond more adequately to Richard and to analyse with him his behaviour, the possible reasons for his feelings of extreme hurt and the effect of his behaviour upon others, without giving him the feeling that she rejects him as a person. Allison knows that the sort of behaviour which she sees as victim behaviour touches her in a vulnerable spot: countertransference. This confrontation makes her conscious again of this old feeling.

The professional conduct and skills of the practitioner

5.5 Empathy

Empathy is the capacity to place oneself in another person's thought-and-feeling world. Empathy does not mean that we have to have gone through what the other person is going through but what it does mean that we are able to be open to the other's experience. In fact, if as practitioners we happen to have had experiences which are similar to those we are hearing about, we need to be careful not to jump to the conclusion that we know what the other is feeling: every person and therefore every experience is different. Empathy consists first and foremost of understanding without analysis, judgment or censure. Empathy invites the other to *experience* feelings; showing empathy, allowing the other to feel what s/he feels, can enable the other to gain insight, to work through grief and anger, or simply to have the experience of being heard and understood.

> Madeleine, who is in her early forties, works in a care home on a unit for both disabled residents and elderly residents who are suffering from dementia. There is a high death rate amongst these residents and this affects Madeleine, although she has built a shield around herself which enables her to cope reasonably well. A moment comes when she begins to be aware of a certain irritation and impatience with the grief which the families of dying residents show, particularly when it involves the daughters of dying or deceased mothers. Thoughts like: 'You've had your mother with you long enough... you don't need to feel all this grief' go through her mind.
>
> Madeleine comes from a large family; she was the ninth child and five more followed her. In the family it is a hard job to keep all the mouths fed and both her parents work very hard indeed. There is little time and attention in their household for the children's joys and sorrows and also very little warmth. Her mother is a silent and slightly remote woman and it feels to Madeleine as if she lives in nomansland.
>
> Once she has married and had her first child, Madeleine and her mother begin to achieve a bit more closeness; her mother has more time now that all the children have left home and over countless cups of tea a mutual feeling of connection steadily grows. For a period of a couple of years

Madeleine is very happy about this. Then, very suddenly, her mother dies. Madeleine is furious and distraught with grief: she feels abandoned and betrayed.

When she is confronted at work with the grief of daughters for the mothers they have lost, she feels anew the abandonment and anger she herself felt, both as a child and as an adult. She is blocked in her ability to offer guidance to daughters who have been able to enjoy their mothers' company all their lives, whereas she only had those two short years...

She is unable to empathize with these women, she just thinks they are ungrateful for all they have received from their mothers. 'Be glad with what you've had from your mother!': this is countertransference.

It is not like Madeleine to feel so angry inside or to react to other people in such a rejecting way. She finds herself unprofessional in this respect and begins a dialogue with herself about it. Gradually she becomes aware of her feelings for her mother and allows the tears to flow. On her own at home she gives herself the chance to grieve properly for her mother and this helps her to conduct herself in a more professional way at work.

Sharon, a young woman of twenty-five, works in a community centre. One of the people on her caseload is the nineteen-year-old Carmen. They get on very well together and things have been going well with Carmen for quite a while; she is following a vocational training and is singing in a band with some other young people in the centre. Carmen has a new boyfriend of twenty-four, with whom she is very much in love, and one day she asks Sharon if she can have a word with her. She tells Sharon that she has caught a sexually transmitted disease from her boyfriend.

Sharon reacts angrily to Carmen, saying 'how could she have been so stupid when everything was going so well and that she'd better dump this boyfriend straight away.' Carmen says that she finds that too harsh and that she loves him; Sharon is disappointed in Carmen and makes no attempt to hide it. It is a very frustrating conversation for both of them: Carmen feels rejected, misunderstood and unsupported. Sharon sits fretting about her reaction until late that evening and when she goes to bed it keeps her awake. She tells her supervisor about it in her next session.

Sharon's father was unfaithful to her mother. He was away a great deal, and when he was there he was a critical and authoritarian presence. For years Sharon fell for the wrong boyfriends, boyfriends like Carmen's. Finally, and with a great deal of effort, Sharon gets her life in order. Carmen confronts her with a part of herself that is still too painful, a part that she doesn't yet have within her control. Her countertransference prevents her from responding empathically to Carmen, who doesn't feel supported by her. During the supervision Sharon experiences how her own powerlessness and anger with herself played a role in her reaction to Carmen. It is a relief to Sharon to be able to speak about this without being criticized for unprofessional behaviour. The next time she sees Carmen, she will speak to her about the conversation they had. She will apologize to Carmen for her angry, unprofessional reaction.

5.6 Sincerity and openness in contact

Sincerity and openness in contact means that as practitioners, counselors or coaches we know how to attune our feelings with our behaviour in a way which invites the client's confidence. There is no acting, no magic tricks, just a genuine interest in and a sincerely felt openness towards the other person and it is this which forms the basis of trust and security which will enable self-reflection. As practitioners we must try as much as possible to think outside our own frame of reference and to become increasingly aware of our own judgments and feelings and also aware that the views and particularly the feelings of the person we are listening to can be and very often are different from our own. Our clients will only feel heard if they are listened to in a spirit of openness; this will help to inspire them towards self-discovery and growth.

Christine, a student of alternative therapy, tells her supervisor about an initial interview with a client during which she experienced an emotional block. The woman was experiencing a variety of physical symptoms which were all stress-related. During the interview she spoke about her husband who had recently confessed to her the extra-marital affair which had already been going on for months. He had also asked her not tell the story to either side of the family, nor to their children, before he had had time to decide what he was going to do.

From that moment on Christine was too personally affected to be able to listen properly. 'What creeps men are!' is what she thought, and worse, and she was no longer in the right state of mind to be able to listen to this woman. She wanted to protect her against this man, to give her advice, to take her by the hand, but she wasn't able to do was to listen to her client's own needs, wishes and limitations. She had simply not heard any more of what had been said.

Christine had a tyrant of a father; he was a cold, remote, sly and aggressive man. Following her parents' divorce when she was still a small child, she was made to go and see him against her will and at times under police pressure. If after one of these obligatory weekends he arrived back with her at her house before the appointed time, he would make her sit in the car outside her mother's front door until he decided it was time. Christine always tried to be perfect in her dress and manners so as not to provoke her father's aggression. Her only expression of resistance was never to call him 'daddy'.

During the supervision it becomes clear that Christine was so deeply affected by her client's grief and powerlessness that she was herself confronted with her own childhood feelings of powerlessness, became emotionally blocked and could therefore no longer listen to what her client needed. She recognizes this as countertransference and she has particular trouble with it in relation to issues about men and sexuality. She finds it difficult to listen sincerely and openly to clients when these issues arise.

At the end of the supervision, Christine asks her supervisor whether she was put off by her shoes; she had intended to change her trainers for a pair of smart shoes before she came out, but she had forgotten to do so. During the session she had wondered several times whether the supervisor was able to take her seriously in these weird shoes: transference. The supervisor looks her up and down and says drily that it was true that the shoes didn't entirely match the colour of her sweater, but that she had personally not been too disturbed by it. She suggests that they pick up the subject of transference and countertransference in the next session.

Ruth works as a psychiatric nurse. During a supervision session she says how extremely irritated she becomes if a client responds to a question she has asked by saying: 'I don't know'. For instance she may be trying to find out if a client's medication is working. She asks: 'Have you had less trouble with fears during the past week?' and the client will say: 'I don't really know.' 'Then I just stop listening, I get annoyed with the client because he won't co-operate,' says Ruth.

This sounds like countertransference, thinks the supervisor and asks: 'How come you can't allow the other person to hesitate or to be indecisive or to take time to work out what he's feeling? How come the other person has to come up with an immediate answer and what is it that makes you lose focus and means you can't be open any more?'

Ruth is convinced that she always has to get things right: she has to excel on her course and achieve high marks – no scraping passes for her. Her work with her clients must go without a single hitch and she is not allowed to make mistakes, so if a client says that he doesn't know exactly what he is feeling, she immediately feels she has failed. 'So, a client is not allowed to hesitate because you don't want to have that feeling?' is a question which she will need to think about.

Ruth's countertransference, her fear of failure and the pain which accompanies it, makes her vulnerable and constrained in her contact with her clients. The fact that already, so early in her career, she has to get everything right, means that she is unable to open herself fully to others. She cannot join the client in looking at what is actually happening. The issue must instantly be clear and manifest, otherwise she gets confused. Ruth is not allowed to learn or 'not to know'; she has to know how to do everything instantly.

Ruth had a mother who from the very beginning took everything over from her because the little girl was not quick enough or didn't do things properly. Because Ruth didn't get the chance to practice and to learn she often didn't know how things worked. By rejecting her uncertainty her mother only reinforced it; she also often corrected her verbally with: 'How is it possible that you don't know *that*?' Her mother gave Ruth a perpetual feeling of failure and this made Ruth feel lonely, angry and sad.

In the course of her supervision, Ruth becomes more aware of her mother's rejection and it makes her re-experience her sadness. She also be-

> comes aware of her own self-rejection and her rejection of people who have doubts. Only when Ruth allows herself to not to know, to learn and to have doubts, will she really be able to be open to her clients and to their uncertainties. She will have to give herself permission to feel as she feels in order to do the same for her clients.

5.7 Confrontation

The qualities of respect, openness, acceptance and empathy are prerequisites for good practice in supervision, coaching and leadership. But as well as the ability to listen with sincerity and to show openness and understanding, it is also important that a professional practitioner is able to 'give back' perceived behaviour to a client or co-worker: in other words to confront and to function as a mirror. In the context of working relationships the ability to give and receive feedback is of inestimable value. Effective confrontation means giving feedback and holding up a mirror to others in such a way that they are willing to look at their own behaviour. The ability to do this is directly connected with the body language, verbal skills and tone-of-voice of the person who is giving the feedback; the one on the receiving end needs to be able to take the feedback on or at least to be willing to learn how to do this. The giving and receiving of feedback is an art and transference and countertransference issues can disturb the confrontation process. People who have difficulty with setting boundaries often find it difficult to give feedback and people who feel easily rejected often find it difficult to receive feedback; what is more, these personality traits are often combined in the same person: people who easily feel rejected often find it difficult, because of this fear of rejection, to confront another person with the behaviour which is bothering them. If people allow others to overstep their limits for too long, the held-in feedback, when finally expressed, will usually not come out in the most constructive of ways; this then means that the chance that the recipient will react positively is reduced and the result is a vicious circle.

A positive but discerning self-image and the capacity for self-reflection are essential if we are to use feedback effectively. Feedback works constructively only when all parties have the willingness and the courage to 'learn'.

Benny works in a rehabilitation centre for young offenders, where he supervises young people with a criminal record. Benny, who has a history of vagrancy and drug-use, just managed to stay out of the hands of the law, which now means that he is on 'the right side of the law' at the centre. He has always had issues with authority. He had a stepfather who was certainly no angel and Benny could do no right in his eyes; his mother all too often sided with her new husband against Benny.

During a work-assessment Benny is told that he gives the boys too much leeway and that he must be more vigilant about the boundaries. Benny is instantly angry with his manager and with his colleagues; they just don't get it! His colleagues are far too harsh and show no sympathy for these boys who've already had such a hard time of it.

Benny was a rejected child; he is scared of pulling the boys into line or of confronting them, scared of being rejected by them, scared that they won't like him if he sets limits. For him setting limits and rejection are one and the same; this is because as a child he was restricted and rejected all the time. He sees himself in the boys he works with and projects onto them his own rejected child. He is unable to embody authority because in his experience authority means rejection, rejection of the child in him: countertransference. His fear of being rejected by the youths in his care and not being liked by them means that he is unable set proper boundaries.

Benny will have to experience and to recognize that authority does not always imply rejection and the most important part of this process will be accepting himself as the child he was: lovable but also difficult, demanding attention in the wrong way because he couldn't get it 'for free'; in this he is probably not very different from his own clients. This insight could well help him, in his guiding role, to see that warmth and clear limits can go hand in hand.

Annabel, still in training as a therapist, is in the process of setting up her own practice. During a supervision session she talks about a consultation which overran by an hour; she found it difficult to send the client away. It emerges that in her private life she also has trouble asking friends to leave if it's late and she wants to go to bed, or to say that she would like an evening on her own or alone with her boyfriend. In their flat they have permanent open-house, a constant coming and going of friends who also regularly join them for dinner. Annabel is afraid of hurting people; she wants to please other people, she says, and this is why she by-passes her own needs and feelings.

As a child Annabel really wanted closeness and warmth from her mother, but her mother didn't see that this is what her daughter needed. Instead, because Annabel clung to her a great deal, she took her to the doctor and said: 'Doctor can you have a look at her, she's been so very clingy recently.' When she's about four her older brother starts to cuddle her a lot, which at first she really likes. But later, when her brother starts to go too far and to violate her boundaries, she is unable to stop him: he doesn't listen to her. Because Annabel's experience is that her mother doesn't listen to her either, it is years before she tells anybody about what has been happening to her. In her relationship she never dares to take the initiative in lovemaking because she is scared that her boyfriend will reject her. She is frightened of being rejected if she asks for cuddles: 'Doctor, my girlfriend has been so very clingy recently'. Added to this she has the ambiguous feeling: 'You seem to want cuddles so much but when you get them from your brother you're still not satisfied'. Need, shame and guilt struggle within her for supremacy.

In further sessions she works on her countertransference issues. Annabel has a fine sense of what her clients need but she tends to identify herself too much with them and can no longer feel her own boundaries; she then cannot ask the questions she would like to ask because she is quick to find them too intimate and as a result goes along with the client too much. She must learn to recognize and acknowledge her boundaries, which she feels but cannot yet assert, and to develop the skill of confronting her client, even if it's just having the courage to say: 'I can see that you still have a lot to tell me but our time is almost up. Shall we make a new appointment very soon?' and daring to say to her friends: 'Okay, guys, I'm off to bed now,' or: 'I'd really like an evening to myself tonight. I love having you around but let's make it another time.'

5.7.1 Confrontation during supervision: an example from daily practice

Melissa has regular supervision as part of her training and teaching practice. After the Christmas holidays her supervisor asks her what kind of a Christmas she's had. Melissa says that she went to midnight mass. 'Disgraceful really,' she adds and starts to change the subject.
'Just a minute,' says her supervisor, 'What makes you say "disgraceful" about midnight mass?'
'Well,' says Melissa, 'that's what people say, isn't it, if you only go once a year? And I'm not even a Catholic.'
'But is that what you think, that it's disgraceful to go to midnight mass once a year, when you're not even a Catholic?'
'No, as a matter of fact I don't. Not really.'
'So do you think it, or don't you, or maybe just a bit?'
'Well no, I don't actually.'
'What makes you say it then, to me?'
'Because lots of people think that.'
'Do you think I think that?'
'I don't know.'
'So you want to be one step ahead and to have said it yourself, in case I do think it, is that right?'
'Yes.'
'You know, Melissa, I don't think that at all. But that's not really the point. Let's imagine I'd said: "Ridiculous that you go to church one time in the year when you're not even a Catholic". If I'd said that, how would you have reacted?'
'I'd have agreed with you.'
'What, even though you don't feel it yourself?'
'Yes. I look up to you and I want you to respect me.'
'But in that case you'd be lying to me, because that is what it amounts to, isn't it?'
'Yes.'
'But I don't respect that, your saying something to me you don't really think, because you think that I might…! Dear me, what a complicated business!'

> 'Yes, it is a bit…'.
> 'It must be so exhausting.'
> 'Yes it is, but it happens without my having to think about it really, because I've been doing it for years.'
> Melissa is a small, vigorous woman in her mid-fifties with an Indonesian background. She has learned never to contradict her parents or other authority figures; she was expected, above all else, to conform. In most situations you were not allowed to show what you were really feeling and most of the time Melissa didn't *know* what she was really feeling; even now she still doesn't know what she feels, or if she does know she hardly dares to show it. The supervisor is important to her and Melissa wants her approval; her transference is that she conforms to what she thinks the supervisor expects of her and in doing this she ignores and by-passes her own opinions and her own wishes. This pattern, which she has developed over the years, makes her vulnerable to relational problems and work-related stress.
>
> Not long after this she says to her supervisor during a session: 'I nearly cancelled today.' It appeared that her parents had suddenly turned op on her doorstep unannounced, just as she was about to get into the car to drive to her session. 'And, you know, my door always has to be open for family…'. And yet she had said, carefully and tactfully, that she had to be somewhere, that she had an appointment. Her parents had immediately put on their coats again, saying: 'Don't worry dear, we only dropped by on the off-chance, of course you have things of your own to do.' To her astonishment there wasn't a problem and she had taken a first step in setting her own boundaries!

By now it is probably obvious: when we look at transference and countertransference we are talking about feelings, wishes, expectations and judgments. We are talking about feelings which are not always conscious but which we can make conscious. Not every professional needs to be aware of transference and countertransference issues, but for a professional practitioner who works with people who are in a dependent position, it is certainly advisable. In this book feelings of all kinds have been discussed, along with the source of these feelings and the visible behaviour through which they manifest themselves. In addition to this the examples from daily practice make clear how many and diverse our lingering child feelings can be and how this diversity in transference feelings can certainly disturb the social processes between people, but can also enrich them immeasurably. It can be infinitely fascinating to discover what it is that moves and motivates other people. A practitioner who shares this conviction will be a genuinely curious, alert and committed guide who is constantly growing and developing new skills and deeper insights and who is able to look afresh and with renewed interest at each person s/he encounters.

A few final notes:

- Transference and countertransference are always there, in every interaction and every encounter.
- Transference and countertransference are allowed to be there.
- Transference which has been made conscious can set a meaningful transformation process in motion.
- Countertransference which has been made conscious can increase the professionalism of the practitioner, counselor, coach, supervisor or manager.

References

Boswijk-Hummel, R. (1997). *Liefde in wonderland.* Haarlem: de Toorts.

Delft, F. en G.J. Wijers (2003). *Therapeutische modellen in de sociaal pedagogische hulpverlening.* Soest: Nelissen.

Kohnstam, R. (1987). *Kleine ontwikkelingspsychologie.* Deventer: Van Lochem Slaterus.

Miller, A. (2003). *Het drama van het begaafde kind.* Houten: M.O.M.

Miller, A. (2008). *The drama of the gifted child.* Basic Books.

About the author

Fee van Delft (1949) studied clinical psychology in Leiden and has worked for many years as a lecturer in psychology in a part-time course, Social Care, for students doing on-the-job training [*beroepsbegeleidende leerweg*] at MBO College West. She also lectures in healtcare and social welfare at the Regional Community College in Amsterdam. Alongside her years as a lecturer, her experience is drawn from treating patients and supervising students. Fee has co-authored works on therapeutic models in educational social work, aggression in educational social work and criminality. She co-wrote the book *De mens in thema's*, wich depicts human lives in terms of themes. She also wrote a book on unusual behaviour and counselling.

Titles authored and co-authored by Fee van Delft:
Aggressie in het sociaal pedagogisch werk
Bijzonder gedrag en begeleiden
Criminaliteit
De mens in thema's
Overdracht en tegenoverdracht
Therapeutische modellen in de sociaal pedagogische hulpverlening